CW01164237

MASTER YOUR BELIEFS:

Can You Stop Doubting Yourself Without Feeling Wrong or Guilty? How Subconscious and Mind Change The Way of Thinking, the Emotions, And the Points Of View of The Real World

Stefan Maidan

© Copyright 2020 - All rights reserved.

The content contained within this book may not be reproduced, duplicated or transmitted without direct written permission from the author or the publisher.

Under no circumstances will any blame or legal responsibility be held against the publisher, or author, for any damages, reparation, or monetary loss due to the information contained within this book. Either directly or indirectly.

Legal Notice:

This book is copyright protected. This book is only for personal use. You cannot amend, distribute, sell, use, quote or paraphrase any part, or the content within this book, without the consent of the author or publisher.

Disclaimer Notice:

Please note the information contained within this document is for educational and entertainment purposes only. All effort has been executed to present accurate, up to date, and reliable, complete information. No warranties of any kind are declared or implied. Readers acknowledge that the author is not engaging in the rendering of legal, financial, medical or professional advice. The content within this book has been derived from various sources. Please consult a licensed professional before attempting any techniques outlined in this book.

By reading this document, the reader agrees that under no circumstances is the author responsible for any losses, direct or indirect, which are incurred as a result of the use of information contained within this document, including, but not limited to, errors, omissions, or inaccuracies.

TABLE OF CONTENTS

INTRODUCTION **6**

CHAPTER 1: THE NATURE OF BELIEFS **8**
  WHAT ARE BELIEFS? 8
  HOW BELIEFS DEVELOP? 11

CHAPTER 2: HOW BELIEFS ARE BORN **14**
  WHERE BELIEFS CAME FROM 14
  A LOT OF WHAT POPS UP PROBABLY WON'T MAKE SENSE 20
  DON'T WORRY ABOUT HIDDEN BELIEFS CONTINUING TO WREAK HAVOC 22

CHAPTER 3: IDENTIFYING YOUR LIMITING BELIEFS **26**
  HOW TO RECOGNIZE LIMITING BELIEFS 26
  SELF-LIMITING BELIEFS DRIVE FEAR 28
  SELF-LIMITING BELIEFS 31
  FEAR OF FAILURE 32
  FEAR OF SUCCESS 32
  FEAR OF JUDGMENT 34

CHAPTER 4: BELIEF AND IDENTITY **38**
  HOW BELIEFS AFFECT YOUR BEHAVIOR AND PERFORM ON YOUR LIFE 38
  CHANGING MY BELIEFS IS EASY AND FUN 39

CHAPTER 5: OVERCOMING YOUR LIMITING BELIEFS **42**
  CHALLENGING AND WEAKENING THE AGED LIMITING BELIEFS 42
  CHANGING OUR NEGATIVE HABITS 45
  YOU NEED TO REMOVE YOUR LIMITING BELIEFS 46
  UPGRADING YOUR BELIEF SYSTEM 49
  A 7-STEP PROCESS TO OVERCOME LIMITING BELIEFS 55
  FINAL TIP 60

CHAPTER 6: INTEGRATING YOUR NEW BELIEFS **62**
  INSTALLING NEW SUCCESS BELIEFS 62
  VITAL SUCCESS ATTITUDES AND BELIEFS WHICH MAKE CHANGE POSSIBLE 63
  EXERCISE: CHANGING BELIEFS 66

CHAPTER 7: BUILDING FUNDAMENTAL BELIEFS **68**
  THE POWER OF BELIEFS 68

CHAPTER 8: HOW YOUR OWN MIND WORKS 74
SUBCONSCIOUS BELIEFS 74

CHAPTER 9: HOW TO GET THE RESULTS YOU WANT 86
HOW TO BREAK THROUGH 86
HOW TO TRANSFORM THE EGO RESPONSE 88
HOW DO YOU SEE THE WORLD? 88
BELIEFS ARE NOT ALWAYS BASED ON LOGIC 89
HOW TO CLEAR THE KINK 91
THE POWER OF YOUR STORY 92
RETOOL YOUR INNER CRITIC 92
HOW YOUR SUBCONSCIOUS REMOVES MENTAL BLOCKS 97
IDENTIFY THE CORE ISSUE 97
HOW CAN YOU TELL IF IT'S REALLY, REALLY, REALLY FINISHED? 101

CHAPTER 10: HOW TO USE YOUR BELIEFS STRATEGY TO REMOVE FEAR 106
ANALYZE & EVALUATE YOUR FEARS 107
TAKE CHARGE OF YOUR FEARS 109
CHANGE YOUR PERCEPTION ABOUT FEAR 111

CHAPTER 11: ALIGNING YOURSELF WITH REALITY 116
ACTION STEP 120
UNCOVERING YOUR ASSUMPTIONS 120
ACTION STEP 121
TESTING YOUR ASSUMPTIONS 122
ACTION STEP 122

CHAPTER 12: KNOW THE TRUTH ABOUT YOURSELF 124
LEARN WHO YOU ARE 124

CHAPTER 13: IDENTIFY YOUR GOALS 130
WHY YOU NEED GOALS 130
HOW LIMITING BELIEFS AFFECT YOUR GOALS 131
GOAL SETTING EXERCISE 132

CONCLUSION 136

Introduction

So Often In life we carry the weight of regret, shame, and guilt of our past. We harbor resentment and anguish over what was. If you remain unaware of the impact your history has on your mind, you allow these hidden shadows of your past to wreak havoc in your present. Even after years of therapy and insight, you can find yourself stuck in a cycle of self-sabotage. These hidden shadows can wreak havoc in relationships, finances and business, while destroying your self-esteem and sense of self-worth. You can be reading this right now and still have no idea how deep the roots of your history have infected your mind. So much energy is wasted blaming, shaming, and complaining about ourselves.

We have heard many times about the power of belief, how it can give the power to people in achieving their dreams. And, how a belief can heal someone or the well-known placebo effect. No one can doubt the power of believe. If you believe you can do it, then you can do it. If you believe you can't do it, you certainly can't do it. Believing has a power to strengthen or weaken a person. Believing can either help or hinder a person to achieve his dream.

But many people admit that they have believed they can be successful, and yet they keep failing and never succeed. They believe they can achieve their dreams, but after all struggle and hard work, they still can't achieve it. What they get is just failures and failures. They believe they can be successful, but why do they keep failing?

Believing has different levels. Many people believe only at the conscious level. Believing at the conscious level is different from believing at the subconscious level. In other words, even you believe you can achieve your dream, but if your subconscious mind doesn't believe it, you will never achieve it.

Many people don't understand that believing at the conscious level is different from believing at the subconscious level. Consciously, you believe you can achieve your dream, but subconsciously, you actually don't believe you can achieve it.

With the help of this book, you are going to go on a journey. On this journey, you are going to discover a lot about yourself. You're going to find out beliefs held by you that are not even your own.

This book will help you set up the beliefs you need, and give you the tools you require, to become successful at whatever you put your mind to. Join me on a lightening-speed journey, where soon you will have your own ninja-hacking skills. Let's search for and find the place where you are fully alive, affecting the world with your gift, and being the great person, you were … where success comes effortlessly, and you are blown away by how rich and fulfilling each day is.

CHAPTER 1:

The nature of beliefs

What Are Beliefs?

Belief is the energy behind the placebo effect. However, this psychological power isn't seen just in remarkable placebo studies and infrequent cases of spontaneous recovery. Your beliefs operate for or from you daily in each area of your life. Beliefs aren't just involved right in the mind-body relationship, but they are also subconscious programs that control your behavior.

Think about beliefs as psychological applications installed in your mind that take in raw information through your perceptions and apply significance to it. If you believed yourself and stated, "My weight has not changed this week," it'd be a frightening fact. But if you lasted, "This implies that this diet does not work and I will never get rid of weight," those wouldn't be details.

You generated beliefs regarding what you believed your results intended, but your thought might have been wrong. Your nutrition program might be quite effective, but you may have underestimated just how much you're eating. You may have gained water weight or increased fresh muscle tissue, boosting weight reduction.

You've beliefs about your surroundings, your behaviors, your abilities, as well as your own identity. As soon as you develop a belief, you are going to act like it is true, and you're going to withstand often or filter out anything that disagrees with it. If it comes to nutrition and diet, a lot of men and women believe in things with an almost religious certainty. Low-carb diets, by way of instance, have valid fat-loss advantages like decreasing appetite and controlling insulin.

Unfortunately, whenever someone is effective with a low-carb diet, they frequently take on dogmatic and erroneous beliefs. For their remaining life, they may look at virtually all carbs as fattening, also because they relied on carbohydrates, not carbs, they frequently feel that calories do not count, a harmful and false belief. But try convincing a previously obese low-carb dieter of this (it is about as simple as getting them to change their faith).

Incidentally, if you are a prosperous high-carb/low-fat dieter, do not gloat too much, since confused beliefs about high-carb/low-fat diets are only as common. Some beliefs are a lot more powerful than others. With the potential exception of religious beliefs, individuality beliefs would be the most powerful of all. It's possible to spot a belief in your individuality by what you say after "I'm." "I'm an overeater" is an identity notion.

Beliefs should be respected and honored, but they must also be inspected carefully. A belief is just a generalization or test in mind. If you opt for the risk that you may think things which are really holding you back, then you have taken the first step toward altering your behavior, your entire body, and your own life.

All of us know that a belief is a confidence or trust in something. But most of us do not realize that beliefs are not necessarily based on a rational ground. Most of our core beliefs are developed during our childhood not supported by logical proofs. They stay in our subconscious and guide our perception and behavior without us knowing it. Our childhood irrational beliefs control most of our behavior even today. Sounds funny?

Our belief system is a cohesive set of mutually dependent beliefs. One belief supports the viability of the other and it proceeds as a chain of beliefs and resulting thoughts and ideas. You can also visualize the belief system as a hierarchical set of beliefs where basic beliefs act as the roots and the dependent thoughts as the child nodes.

Our core beliefs are self-explanatory and primitive in nature. These beliefs stand strong without the support of other beliefs.

Our belief system acts as a filter through which we process our experience and perceive the outer world. It is through this filter that we act upon our surrounding in return.

In simple words it is due to our beliefs that the things, situations, experiences make sense to us and it is our beliefs that govern the way we behave. We are what we believe ourselves to be (so true is the statement).

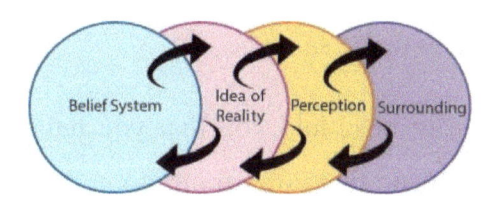

How Beliefs develop?

Our belief system started developing since when we did not even know what thoughts and ideas are. As a kid we started perceiving incidents through the filter of belief system which further resulted into formation of interconnected beliefs. Our beliefs don't demand logic to support them. Rather, they are fuelled up by feelings and emotions. Think of a situation in your childhood when you had accidently broken a cup or your father's pair of glasses and your mother scolded you saying, you are very troublesome and a spoilt brat. A kid's mind after a few similar repetitive situations would begin creating beliefs like, 'I am not good enough' or 'I cannot do a thing properly'.

These events bore no inherent meanings, but the mind had to make sense out of them. It had to give the event a meaning. Anybody would infer such situation in a negative manner. Although, your parents never meant to make you feel inferior and there could have been several other meanings drawn out of the same situation, we kept clinging to the negative core beliefs we developed.

Later in our life, we tend to see the same belief taking form of our reality. We keep attaching every subsequent similar situation with the same meaning, with the same belief.

Although, when your boss told you that you have messed up with the work, it didn't mean that you cannot do it, or you are incapable. You could have also drawn an inference that you were not able to do it at this time but next time you will certainly do it.

But this fails to happen as our childhood beliefs have been weaving our perception. We see what there in our minds is already. We add meaning to the events that support our existing beliefs. We ignore all such events that contradict the rigid beliefs already established in our minds and thus, we more and more believe in it. We see a reality which is not outside but only in our beliefs.

Most of our core beliefs are developed in our childhood as a result of the impactful incidents, our parents' behavior, language and environment. All our beliefs are formed this way, either positive or negative. However, we are aiming at eliminating the negative core beliefs as positive ones are working on our side.

We form negative beliefs adding sense to the events which continue to act as a source of demoralization throughout our lives. The most ridiculous part of this is we live holding on to concepts that are not even real. And these concepts and beliefs make us what we are and what our life is.

CHAPTER 2:

How beliefs are born

Where Beliefs Came From

It is important to remember all the crappy beliefs you picked up over time *aren't* yours. They didn't come from you. There is no way they can ever truly originate within us, because 'big' us is pure positive energy, and knows what's up, as far as this whole conscious creation thing goes.

You picked up on all sorts of vibrations while you were still in the womb. You picked up beliefs based on what your parents believed, on what they told you to be true. They let you know 'how it is' and you took them at their word.

You observed all sorts of things that led you to draw various conclusions about how things worked in the world, what was true, and what wasn't true. And because 99.99 percent of people are operating with all sorts of screwy beliefs, most of what you witnessed, wasn't very encouraging.

All sorts of things happened, that led you to draw various conclusions about yourself, your capabilities and what is possible for you. Unfortunately, most of these conclusions are really crappy.

And you probably think you are broken, and fucked up, in a variety of ways, and perhaps there is no hope for you.

And please don't believe that...there is always hope. When you truly begin to understand we do create our reality, you realize that there is *no way* this can actually be true.

You might not buy in one million percent on the deepest levels of your being, but something gets sparked within, and it starts to permeate. So long as you commit to making the shifts, and just don't give up when you don't get what you want within 48 hours of deciding you want it, you're good to go. But I digress...

Your limiting beliefs didn't just come from your parents and what you may have observed in your immediate environment. There are also beliefs that pervade your culture, and you being part of said culture, absorbed them.

For example, if you come from a culture where women are expected just to serve their men, have babies, and take care of the house, you probably have a hard time believing you can be a successful entrepreneur. You may think your desire is even inappropriate or flat out 'wrong.' You may believe you just aren't capable.

Global and cultural beliefs weren't borne of any personal experience you had that led you to make a certain conclusion or decision. Though you likely had many personal manifestations that mirrored them back to you, because you also believed these beliefs, to some degree.

It is important to remember we can't manifest anything that we aren't a match to *personally*. So, no matter how much energy a belief has behind it, and no matter how many people believe it, you won't be affected if you don't harbor this belief. No one can create in another person's reality.

When it really starts to sink in, our world is created from the inside out, we realize it was the beliefs that caused the experiences. And the experiences further cemented the beliefs, which led to more experiences that mirrored them back. We essentially created a vicious circle.

But now that you know what's up, you can break that most unhelpful pattern of events.

Some beliefs may never be fully shifted, like those big global beliefs that may cause fear. You may never be totally free of fear of nuclear war, terrorist attacks, the financial system collapsing and so on.

You'll probably continue to harbor beliefs that will lead to 'negative' manifestations. And these manifestations will alert you to said beliefs, that you didn't realize had so much energy behind them, because they weren't in your conscious mind much of the time.

But it was there in the background. If we were to maintain conscious awareness of EVERY belief, we have about EVERYTHING, we could not function.

But whatever you manifest, you'll do what you need to do to improve the situation. You'll get lots of helpful insights that will help you move forward. You now know the ball is in your court.

Bottom line—don't make achieving some 'perfect' vibration and 'perfect' life the end goal.

You've Set Some Intentions and Now the Fun Begins...

You have to believe you can have it, like truly believe it. And if you don't, you have to do something about that.

Here's the thing that is really important to remember about law of attraction: again, it's not a tool. It's not an option you can employ in lieu of having no control over your reality. It is something that just 'is' and you have been creating this whole time.

But up until the point you found this out, you were doing it by default; you weren't doing it consciously. You had all sorts of beliefs--not all of them negative--that led to a whole mix of experiences. You have likely had lots of beliefs that served you very well and led to all sorts of positive manifestations.

We are designed to create our experience. Now you are moving into becoming a *deliberate* creator. You now realize the power your thoughts, beliefs and feelings have. And you will work on bringing them in harmony with what you want, rather than having them contradict it.

And being this deliberate creator means diving in and seeing what has been happening internally. You can't be more deliberate in creating your experience, if you have no idea what is holding you back, from allowing what you want into your life.

We don't like facing stuff that makes us feel badly, because well...it feels badly. We prefer to push it down. But again, if you want to be a *deliberate* creator of your life experience, you really don't have a choice. You can't fix something you won't acknowledge is broken.

So, what limiting beliefs do you have around what you want? Sit for a moment and think about something you want to manifest. What is coming up for you? What feelings are rising to the surface? It might be helpful to write this stuff down.

You may think about how no one in your family was every successful, or had money, and you doubt it is possible for you—it's just not in the cards, perhaps. You may think about how you don't have enough money to start a business. You may think about your bad credit, and how you'll never get a loan.

Maybe you want to manifest a *great* relationship. Notice how I said great. The point of working consciously with your energy is to create the most awesome versions of the stuff you want.

You just don't want *any* relationship. You don't want to settle; you don't want to end up with someone who is 'good enough.' You don't want to be with someone who is actually a terrible match for you. But because you are terrified of being alone, you rationalize, justify, and deny various aspects of the person, and relationship, until the cows come home.

There I go digressing again…I do that a lot. Sorry. But when a helpful nugget pops in that I think is somewhat relevant, I just can't help myself. Look I did it again! Okay, back to limiting beliefs for real this time.

So, you start thinking about this great relationship you want with all your heart. And again, these thoughts aren't making you feel so great. You don't start feeling excited that your desire has been created energetically, and you just have to allow it to come to you.

Maybe you start thinking of all the times you have been rejected by people who seemed like really good matches, and it makes you feel like the type of people you would like to date, will never want to date you.

One thing that commonly happens is you begin to have memories of certain events that may not be related to the issue at hand. For example, you are thinking about a relationship, but have some memory of something your teacher said to you in the 5th grade that made you feel badly.

What happens when you sit with resistance, and limiting beliefs, is you will be delivered all sorts of information that matches what you are feeling now. So, it is very relevant. There is a common thread in there as far as your emotions and beliefs go. Anything popping in means something, so don't dismiss any of it.

A Lot of What Pops Up Probably Won't Make Sense

Here's the thing about limiting beliefs...many of them don't make a whole lot of sense to you when you actually identify what they are. They may seem silly, irrational, child-like and what not.

We tend to throw up eye rolls at the various cliches of personal growth because they seem so obvious. But as for having actually considered these points and evaluated our experience against these backdrops...not so much. So, bear with me.

If you dismiss a belief for seeming dumb, illogical, irrational or whatever, and you don't do any work on it, it isn't going anywhere. It will remain stuck in your energy and will continue to serve as the source of a variety of unwanted manifestations. It will continue to cockblock, what you actually want.

Yes, many of these beliefs will seem strange to you as an adult. But that little part of you is still in there, believing that crap. It didn't know any better. It didn't have the capacity to question.

Anything that comes up for you has significance...if it didn't , you wouldn't even have thought about it. All of this information is coming from within. A limiting belief you actually don't have, wouldn't cross your mind, because it has never been in your mind in the first place.

You will also find when you really get down to the nitty gritty of what you believe, it will be absolute. I ***never*** get what I want. People ***always*** screw me over. I ***never*** get respect. Things ***never*** work out for me. As soon as things start going well, something ***always*** pops up that goes wrong.

Given the huge range of experiences you have had, it is highly unlikely things have actually played out in such a black-and -white-fashion. But again, beliefs aren't rational.

Once you start doing this vibrational detective work, you may come to realize how many fucked up beliefs you have, that have been standing in the way of all the awesome things you want. And this may lead you to feel a bit discouraged.

You may even panic a bit. You'll think there is no way you can work through all this garbage, you're totally screwed, and destined to live out your days at the mercy of your crappy beliefs, because they are just too powerful to be brought down.

Don't worry. That isn't going to happen. Yes, it can be a bit disconcerting to see what has really been going on in that mind of yours all this time. It can be quite shocking, and eye-opening, to see how you have been primarily focusing your energy this whole time.

Around now is the time when you will want to beat yourself up for being so stupid, and blaming yourself, for all the unwanted crap in your experience. Do your best to minimize this as much as possible.

Yes, our experience is a response to our vibration. Everything that we have attracted is our 'doing.' But, what do you expect when we have had no freaking idea how things really worked, and we had no freaking clue what we were doing?

When we were kids, especially, we had no idea what was happening. But now that you know what is going on, you can fix it...all of it.

It is also important to remember that no matter what crap has cemented itself into that brain of yours, and no matter what transpired as a result, *you already are* the person who is capable of having exactly what you want. That higher -vibing version of yourself is already within. You don't have to create some whole new version of yourself. You just have to clear out the gunk standing in the way of Who You Are.

It is like a dirty window. You clean off all the grime, and there is the gleaming, shining glass that was there all along.

Don't Worry about Hidden Beliefs Continuing to Wreak Havoc

When you start realizing you have had all these beliefs of which you were not fully aware, there is the tendency to worry there are all these other horrible beliefs you may *never* uncover.

They will remain deep in your subconscious, fucking with you at every turn. And because you'll never find them, you'll always be at their mercy. You won't ever get what you want.

When you find yourself struggling, you'll be convinced there must be some belief that hasn't been uncovered, that is responsible for all your woe, and is keeping what you want from making its way in.

Here's the thing. There is, without a doubt, many beliefs you have that you are not consciously aware of at this very moment. It is highly unlikely you will uncover *every* belief you have about ***everything***.

But for most of us, the beliefs that are getting in the way of creating our more desired reality are quite obvious, and we are very well aware of them.

Feeling like you can't be rich because you have always been poor. Feeling like hard work is necessary to get what you want, you have to suffer, and there is no easier way. Feeling like you can't find a great relationship, because your love life up until this point, has consisted of a parade of assholes.

Is it possible there are some beliefs you may not be aware of right this second that could be tempering your manifestations? For example, starting to make more money, but not as much as you would ideally like to make? Quite possibly. But, at some point, you will discover it. Then you can keep moving along your merry way to creating all sorts of awesomeness.

I don't necessarily believe there are things in our mind that are truly, truly hidden from us. It is more that we just haven't turned our attention towards them and examined them yet.

And the beauty of the law of attraction is that, if there is something standing in your way of improving your life, it will bring you a manifestation that will help you uncover that something.

So, don't worry about some hidden belief screwing with you. Focus on the beliefs you are fully conscious of and may still be a bit stronger than you would like.

CHAPTER 3:

Identifying your limiting beliefs

How to Recognize Limiting Beliefs

Some beliefs are a part of the conscious awareness, but the beliefs that restrict you are typically ones that you do not understand you've. Even if you comply with an effective training and nutrition plan, limiting beliefs working under the surface will result in self-sabotage. Limiting beliefs have to be awakened, ripped out, and replaced since only then have you ever coped with the exact cause of several body fat issues at the origin. Flushing out restricting beliefs requires honest self-analysis.

Begin by asking yourself these questions:

☐ What causes me to become obese?

- What is preventing me from becoming thinner?

If you listen closely to your answers, you might hear restricting beliefs mentioned as cause-and-effect or if-then relationships.

For instance:

"I am overweight and cannot get leaner because..."

- That I don't have any motivation.
- I don't have any willpower.
- I've got a slow metabolism.
- I hate exercise.
- I really like food.
- I am hurt.
- I overeat when I am stressed.
- I really don't understand exactly what to eat or how to cook.
- If you are over fifty, then it is too late.
- When I have one sting, I cannot stop.
- When you have children and a job, then there is no opportunity to work out.
- If I try and fail, then I will hate myself.

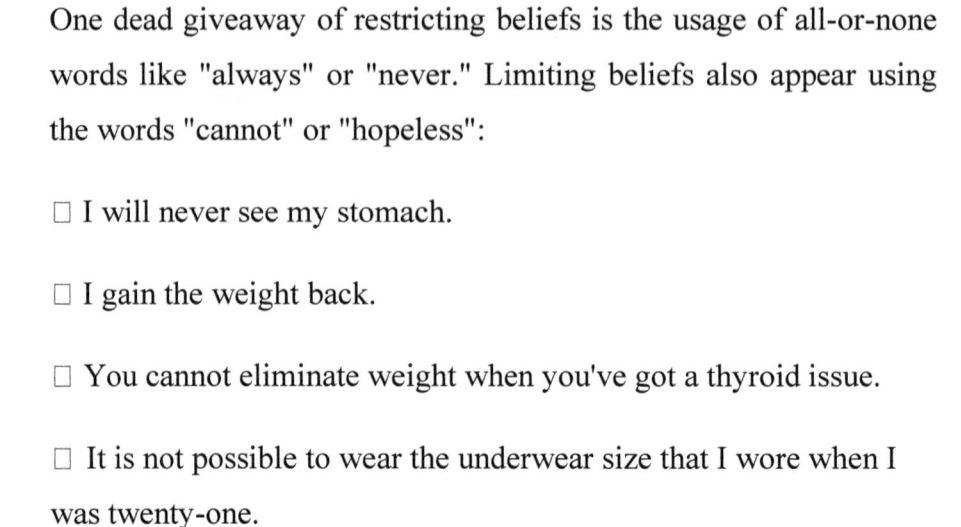

One dead giveaway of restricting beliefs is the usage of all-or-none words like "always" or "never." Limiting beliefs also appear using the words "cannot" or "hopeless":

☐ I will never see my stomach.

☐ I gain the weight back.

☐ You cannot eliminate weight when you've got a thyroid issue.

☐ It is not possible to wear the underwear size that I wore when I was twenty-one.

Self-Limiting Beliefs Drive Fear

Our fears and anxiety are the most obvious factor in determining our self-limiting beliefs.

It's vital that we examine this topic because we need to be able to identify fearful and anxious thinking before we can identify which thoughts are our self-limiting beliefs.

It's more comfortable to ask, "What am I afraid of" than it is to ask, "What is holding me back?"

I will also connect the dots between our fears and our self-limiting beliefs. Not only will I cover this, but I will discuss the most common fears.

These are the fears that most commonly hold us back in life—the self-limiting fears that keep us from reaching our fullest potential.

Fear

Fear is an actual physiological response to external danger.

Fear is healthy; it has allowed humans to survive over the countless generations of existence here on this earth.

For example, if we were to see a substantial predatory animal, our human instinct would be to feel threatened.

The natural fear response would be an increase in our adrenaline, often causing symptoms that range from our heart racing, our hands sweating, and a sudden urge and ability to run away—and run fast!

Anxiety

Anxiety, on the other hand, is psychologically based. In other words, when a person is anxious, their thought processes are causing their anxiety. This can be as simple as worrying or obsessively dwelling on a thought or thoughts that cause an individual to react or respond in a number of negative ways—whether consciously or subconsciously. The critical thing to remember is that these thoughts are often not based in truth, or, too often, we're giving them too much value.

It's the thoughts and messages that we give ourselves that cause anxiety. It's important to recognize in ourselves what those fears are and why we have them.

Self-Limiting Beliefs

Self-limiting beliefs are the things we tell ourselves about who we are. These negative beliefs lead to negative feelings about ourselves. When we feel negative about ourselves, it's impossible to develop confidence in who we are and what we're trying to accomplish. It's also impossible to love ourselves.

When we don't believe in ourselves or what we're doing, or even love ourselves, it shows in our attitude. It affects everything in our lives. It doesn't just affect our success, but it also affects our relationships.

By understanding this, we can come to understand why the saying, "You can't love someone until you love yourself," rings with truth. We may try, but if our attitude isn't working, neither will our relationships.

The reason behind this is because our attitude affects our actions. We may feel that we love someone, but our negative attitude causes us to say or do hurtful things toward that person. So, the question is, how do we fix this negative cycle?

The answer lies in our thoughts. If we change our thoughts, we change our beliefs, which changes our feelings, which then leads to changing our attitude, and finally—our actions.

Below is a diagram of how this sequence works.

Fear of Failure

If you have a fear of failure, you may be able to recognize yourself thinking or saying things like:

"What if I don't do it, right?"

"I'm just not good at this."

The fear of failure is a common fear shared by those of us that tend to have the characteristic of perfectionism. Perfectionism can be a useful tool, but it can also be a detrimental characteristic.

Other phrases you may notice yourself thinking or saying may sound something like this:

"What if I lose…"

"What if I don't have…"

Fear of loss is directly related to our fear of failure. It's not hard to recognize that success requires risk. If we carry around a fear of loss, we understand that "failing" may mean "loss."

Fear of Success

If you're afraid of success, you may notice yourself thinking or saying phrases that coincide with the following statements:

"What if I'm given even more responsibility?"

"I can't handle being in the spotlight…."

"I can't handle that much pressure…."

This line of thinking is *fearing the responsibility and vulnerability* that success can bring you. In truth, this is a reality for successful leaders.

You may also find yourself thinking or saying other phrases if you're afraid of success, such as:

"I couldn't make all those changes."

"I can't sacrifice_____."

"I can't change who I am."

"My feelings are who I am."

Fear of change is understandable. It is also directly related to success. The truth is, you cannot make improvements to your life, if you're not willing to make improvements to the way you think and act. This requires change. Change can be difficult because it's uncomfortable. Because making changes can lead to discomfort, it can also be related to the *fear of emotional pain.*

The last set of beliefs you may find yourself expressing through thoughts or words may be along these lines:

"What if_____happens…"

"What if I don't like who I become?"

"What if it doesn't turn out the way I expect it to?"

These phrases are also related to *fear of the unknown*. Many of us find comfort in trying to plan things. We can try to plan anything and everything. This may be anything ranging from our circumstances to the responses of others. We're afraid of the unknown, so, we mentally start planning how we want it turn out. Granted, there's nothing wrong with visualizing success—more on this in a later chapter. What gets us in trouble is expecting a result and not being able to respond appropriately when it's not the result we wanted. This is deeply rooted in our need for control in order to feel secure. The problem with this type of thinking is that we can never have absolute control over our circumstances. We absolutely have no control over others. Any time we try to control, we're causing unhealthy resentments inside ourselves and others.

Fear of Judgment

Those of us who have a fear of being judged may have thoughts along the lines of:

"What will they think of me?"

"What if _____ doesn't like me?"

"What if I embarrass myself?"

"No one understands me or what I'm going through."

"No one could ever love me."

"If they knew the real me, they would never like me."

The fear of judgment comes from a deep need for approval of others. It's also related to *fear of rejection,* or *fear of abandonment.* With fears of judgment or rejection, we may think that no one understands what we're going through; we believe that our baggage, so to speak, is different from that of others'. Because we may believe that our baggage is too much, we feel that no one could ever love us. This fear often follows us around when we're holding onto deep shame and guilt. Being vulnerable with others is scary in itself because we think that if they knew about all the shameful things we've done or been through, we would never be accepted. If we believe this about ourselves, if often shows up in our relationships. We may talk to our friends a lot, but never truly connect in an authentic way. We may also be afraid of becoming emotionally intimate with our loved ones or significant other. This may stem from a very memorable experience of ours when we were hurt by someone we trusted. Whatever the reason, we may justify it and never experience deep and meaningful relationships because of this fear.

We may put too much value on what others think about what we're doing. We may have a *fear of humiliation.* We may never go after what we want because of the fear of making a mistake and embarrassing ourselves. On the other end of this fear, if we tend to dwell on fears of abandonment or being alone, we may come on too strong to others in our relationships. We may crave constant touch, attention, or conversation. We must identify the thoughts and self-limiting beliefs we tell ourselves that are driven by our fears if we are to gain the tools to act toward overcoming these beliefs successfully. Before moving forward, I strongly encourage you to go to your local dollar store and purchase a blank journal or notebook. Utilize this tool to note your behaviors and attitudes that you feel have negative consequences. Next, write down all of the thoughts and beliefs you hold onto about yourself or your life, whether positive or negative. By doing this, you can start to analyze who you are today. Realistically, you won't be able to write down all the thoughts and beliefs you have in one sitting, or even in one day. You may not be able to do this right away for your actions either, especially if you're not in the habit of being self-aware.

CHAPTER 4:

Belief and identity

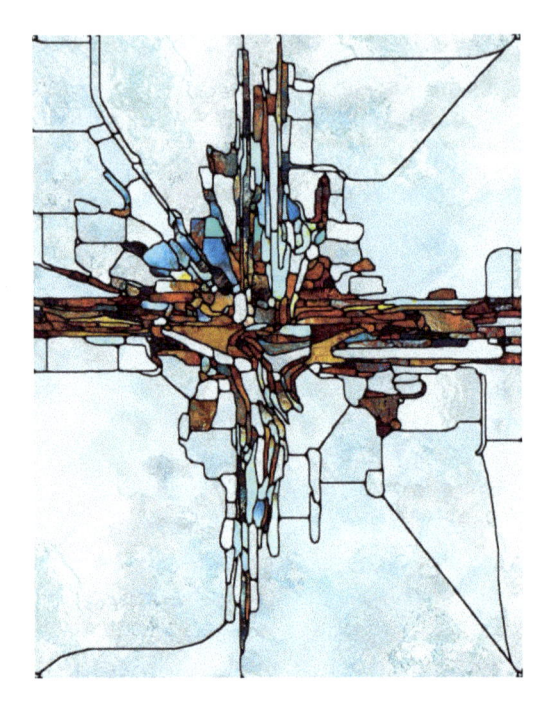

How Beliefs Affect Your Behavior and Perform on Your Life

In case you do not think something is possible, you generally won't try it. If you attempt while your mind is obsessed with doubts, then you won't work well, and you are very likely to stop at the first obstacle. With exotic holidays or tens of thousands of dollars in prize money dangled as incentives, these competitions have become hugely popular, and you would think they would supply all of the motivation you would have to attain the best shape of your life.

The attrition figures tell another story—many people who enter those competitions never complete.

People can say that they believe in something, but that is their conscious mind talking. Behavior is the genuine expression of what individuals believe on the subconscious level.

Everything you think is possible, and everything you think you are capable of will influence what jobs you try and if you persist through hardship or contribute up. What you think will influence every behavior and decision you make every day. Some folks will not eat particular foods due to their religious customs. Some people do not eat meat because they think it is unethical to kill creatures.

If you strongly appreciate your wellbeing, and if you feel that eating fruits and vegetables will provide you unbounded power and vitality, you then won't need to drive yourself to eat them; you'll crave them. If doing something violates your values and beliefs, then it'll be from the question.

Changing my beliefs is easy and fun.

This is extremely important to understand and is one statement that can be the difference between succeeding in life and not succeeding, so I really need you to see how important it is.

Seriously, if you mentally skip over this, you will hinder your progress in life drastically.

Okay, I think you now know how important this is.

I would like you to repeat over and over in your head as much as possible for the next few days:

One of the biggest lies we unconsciously tell ourselves is that change is hard, life is hard, relationships are hard, and doing something new is hard; it's all too difficult. With this frame of mind, we never get anything done. We don't take the first step, and we forget about our dreams, our goals, and our ambitions in life. You deserve an amazing life, you deserve money, love, a great job, and that amazing feeling of happiness.

There is a lot more to changing a belief than reciting an affirmation over and over, of course, and depending on the belief, some are much easier to install than others.

Do you need to become a part of the community? Certainly not. But studies have shown that belonging to a community, even if it is online, makes change much easier than going it alone. Still, this is entirely your decision.

CHAPTER 5:

Overcoming your limiting beliefs

Challenging and Weakening the Aged Limiting Beliefs

Limiting beliefs incorporate some excuse that is holding you any notion preventing you from doing it. When you've recognized a limiting belief, the next step is to battle it. Strong beliefs aren't always easy to eliminate. But, despite deeply held beliefs, the challenge procedure can weaken them. By questioning your older beliefs, you produce doubt, and that is all of the openings you want to slide an empowering fresh belief in its own place.

Challenge the Belief Directly

The very first means to break a limiting belief would be to question its validity. Place that impression onto the witness stand and "cross-examine" it as though you're a prosecuting lawyer in a court. Find evidence, build your case, and establish that it isn't correct.

Challenge the Belief by Questioning the Source

To prevent becoming a victim of your own limiting beliefs, then you have to do exactly the identical thing and challenge them by questioning the origin. Can you choose them? Were they passed down from police, parents, or friends? Have you ever been tried to live your whole life based on somebody else's belief system? Sometimes the mere understanding that a belief isn't yours is sufficient to ruin it.

Challenge the Usefulness of this Belief

During your lifetime, you chose up beliefs that never served you; however, you have held them since. You also embraced beliefs that served you in one time, like during youth, but they dropped their usefulness. Ask yourself: Why does this view serve any helpful function? Has this notion ever prevented me from becoming something that I desired? Does this belief aid me or hurt me? Whether this opinion hurts me personally, limits me personally, serves no helpful function, or prevents me from becoming what I need, then how fast can I eliminate it?

Challenge the Belief by Weighing the Consequences

Motivation does not come just from benefits and rewards (the carrot). For a lot of men and women, pain or outcome (the rod) is a much greater incentive. Recognizing consequences may be the last nail in the coffin of old limiting beliefs. When you think about a belief that is restricting you, ask yourself: Which will be the consequences of maintaining it? What's this cost me previously? What does it cost me now? What's going to be the future impact if I do not change this today?

Your Past Does Not Have to Be a Part of Your Present

If we are being honest with ourselves, each of us wishes to reach our highest potential. If you were to rate each area of your life, on a scale from 1-10, how would you rate your career, relationships, spirituality, health, environment, and education? Journal this now!

Fears Have Origins

Our deepest fears have origins. All of the common, deep, emotional self-limiting fears we have—they're all rooted in an event or events early in our childhood. Before you set this part aside as some psychological mumbo-jumbo, I must insist—it's true! I'll give you my own example so that you can see the correlation.

Events Trigger Fear

If we can trace our fears back from early events, we can definitely find correlations between events that happen to us that tend to trigger certain thoughts, or fearful self-limiting beliefs. If you're still finding you're acting out in any way that bothers you or others, I highly encourage you to write down the event preceding these behaviors.

Maybe you don't act out; maybe you simply find yourself having a bad attitude in regard to certain incidents. Be careful. Any negative thinking can lead to a negative attitude and, ultimately, destructive behaviors. I

Changing Our Negative Habits

When we ask the "what if" questions for too long, we start to answer them in a negative way. We start to expect the worse and, therefore, believe it—but that's not necessarily true. The next step here is to identify your negative habits.

First, here is re-cap of mine from the previous examples.

My fearful self-limiting beliefs were behind my actions of:

• Quitting things too soon or running away from challenges

• Not taking any action even when I knew I needed to

• Making decisions based on fear, decisions I would later regret

• Missing out on great opportunities and experiences I could have otherwise enjoyed

• Missing out on authentic relationships

• Being self-centered and unable to love others and fully enjoy their company

It's your turn. From the events you journaled about, add an additional journal entry for the negative habits that accompany them. To gain from this entry, you must be completely honest with yourself. Once you've done that, you can move on to how we change our negative habits.

In order to change our habits or our recurring behaviors, we must replace them. This is similar to our thoughts. For example, we cannot get rid of a thought by decided to stop thinking it. In order to get rid of a negative thought, we must replace it with a positive thought. This is why positive affirmations are so powerful. Using affirmations is the art of transforming our thinking. Similarly, our habits work the same way. If we want to change our negative habits, we must replace them with a positive habit. There's a catch, though. It's very easy to replace a negative habit we wish to get rid of with another negative habit. There is a joke in recovery that when we kick one addiction, we pick another to take its place. It rings with some truth, though. This is where we have to get creative and be mindful about what we're replacing our current habits with.

You Need to Remove Your Limiting Beliefs

Why do you need to remove your limiting beliefs? If you really want to achieve your dream and be successful, you need to remove a block within you that called limiting beliefs.

We can achieve our dreams quickly if we have beliefs that support us. Empowering beliefs will trigger positive emotions such as motivated, passionate, courageous, persistent, *etc.* As we learned before, positive thinking only works for those who are emotionally positive. So, if you have empowering beliefs, plus positive thinking, your life will be truly amazing. Achieving your dream and becoming successful are just a matter of time.

But what if you have limiting beliefs? Limiting beliefs will trigger negative emotions and you will behave congruently with it. For example, a limiting belief will trigger a feeling of lazy and makes you procrastinate. You need to do your job, but your subconscious mind makes you to feel lazy, then you tell yourself that you will do it tomorrow.

Laziness, fear, procrastinate, nervous, and other negative feelings are triggered because of limiting beliefs. We are often taught to get rid of those feeling using willpower.

To deal with negative emotions, we need to enter into the source, the subconscious mind. Then we persuade it, so it is willing to remove limiting beliefs inside us. Limiting beliefs often put someone into a dead end when they want to make changes.

You have to identify whether you have a limiting belief or not. If you don't have a limiting belief, what you need to remove?

The easiest way in identifying limiting beliefs is to be honest when looking at your achievement. Are you satisfied with all your achievements? Are you satisfied with what you have now? If you are not satisfied, have you ever tried to achieve something higher, but always failed to achieve it?

You might want to have a higher income. You tried to earn more money, you set a goal and tried to achieve it, but you always failed to achieve it, many times. Moreover, you can see a similar pattern.

You always ended up failing in the same hole. Have you ever experienced it? If yes, it is an indication of limiting belief.

Then ask yourself the following questions:

1. I want to achieve (your goal), but_____.

2. I can't get (your desire), because_____.

3. I want to be able to do (skills you want to master), but_____.

The answers of those questions are your limiting beliefs.

A program, as long as it doesn't hinder or hurt you, then you don't need to change or modify it. Some people, after learning about limiting beliefs, were so actively looking for their limiting beliefs, and even came to complain, "Why I can't find my limiting beliefs? What's wrong with me?" What's wrong with you is you keep looking for something you don't have. If you can't find it, that means you don't have it. Concerning can't find a limiting belief can create a new limiting belief.

You don't have to do anything if everything goes as you plan and hope for. Enjoy your life. If you feel a block or a resistance when you want to achieve something higher, that is when you have to make changes. If you want to achieve your dream, but you feel lazy, fear, or other uncomfortable feelings, that is when you have to identify your limiting beliefs. After finding it, you have to remove it.

The main point is when you have set a higher goal, act your plans, and you can achieve your goal, then you don't have limiting beliefs. But if when you set a goal, but you feel uncomfortable with it, then it is an indication of limiting beliefs. You have to identify, after that you have to remove it, or it will keep hindering or sabotaging you.

Upgrading Your Belief System

Changing your belief system

You can't go the extra mile and transform your life without changing your belief system. Think of your belief system as a program that runs in the background without your knowledge. It determines what's possible for you.

Your programming (belief system) leads you to have specific thoughts; these thoughts generate emotions, and these feelings compel you to take particular actions. Eventually, what you do determines the results you get in life.

Most people have fully formed belief systems once they reach adulthood, and they usually keep the same ones for the rest of their lives. They never change their beliefs regarding the world. Their political opinions remain the same, their vision of themselves stays static, and their religious beliefs never change. They seldom question what they believe, and instead behave as if their views are entirely correct. That assumption couldn't be further from the truth.

The origins of your belief system

Your current belief system was created based on past information you received from parents, teachers, or the media. You accepted them as true on a subconscious level because you weren't in a position to choose to reject them. Your belief system is also the result of beliefs you formed due to emotionally charged experiences, such as a childhood trauma.

Fortunately, you now have the power to choose what to believe and can eliminate any belief that has become irrelevant. The limiting ideas that have been holding you back could be about money, relationships, spirituality, or even yourself. Life is about getting rid of limiting beliefs and adopting new, empowering ones that will help you move forward. See your belief system as a costume you wear. If you don't like it, change it.

What's your personal story?

What is your current belief system? How does it impact the decisions you make? Is it limiting you or is it empowering you?

Your personal story works similarly. Buy into the wrong narrative, and it can make your life miserable.

Change it, and you'll suddenly feel empowered. A few years from now you could even find yourself achieving things that you didn't even think were possible.

So, what's your story? Is it the story of a hero or heroine who's moving towards their goals with confidence and excitement? Or is it the story of a victim who feels powerless?

If you want to transform your life, you need to take an honest look at your personal story and make a firm commitment to rewrite it in a way that better suits your vision. You are what you believe, so don't buy into anyone else's beliefs. Choose your own and do so carefully!

Remember: Your beliefs are a scenario you can rewrite, a costume you can change, an identity you can alter.

So what about you? How strong are your beliefs?

When it comes to success, your beliefs are one of the most critical factors. They are what will drive your actions and determine your level of perseverance. They can be the difference between an average person and an exceptional one.

Think of the most significant dream you have. Do you genuinely believe you can achieve it, or do you hope that one day, if you're lucky, you might attain it?

Would you be willing to bet $100 that you'll make your dream come true? What about $1,000 or $10,000? What does your answer say about your level of certainty?

What's holding you back?

Why haven't you achieved the results you want in life? What's holding you back?

You must have written your story in a way that prevents you from living the life you want. There must be a set of specific beliefs that are working against you. What are they?

Below are some examples of common limiting beliefs you may currently hold:

I don't know the right people.

I don't have enough time.

I don't have enough money.

I'm not smart enough.

I'm too shy.

I'm not confident enough.

I don't have any talent.

I won't be happy until such and such happens.

There's too much competition.

I'm too old.

I'm too young.

I don't know how to do it.

And the list goes on and on.

How to identify your limiting beliefs

To discover your limiting beliefs, look at each area of your life and ask yourself why you aren't where you want to be. Then list your reasons.

Check out the example below:

1. Why aren't I where I want to be regarding finances?

I'm not smart enough.

I don't have enough time to work on my side business.

Money is the root of all evil.

2. Why haven't I attracted the man or woman of my dreams?

I'm not attractive.

I'm disinteresting.

I need money to attract a partner.

I don't have the time to go out.

I don't like parties.

3. Why don't I have the career I want?

I don't have the right education.

I don't know the right people.

I don't know what I need to do.

I don't have enough time.

My friends and family aren't supportive.

Do you hold any of the limiting beliefs mentioned above?

Using your emotions to identify your beliefs

You can pinpoint your limiting beliefs by investigating specific feelings that you experience on a consistent basis. Do you feel angry on a regular basis? Do you feel sad? Do you feel frustrated? If so, ask yourself this: What would I need to believe to feel that emotion?

The negative emotions you experience are the result of your beliefs. You feel a certain way because you have certain assumptions or expectations regarding how things should be. When things aren't the way you want them to be, you suffer.

A 7-step process to overcome limiting beliefs

Challenging your limiting beliefs

When you believe something, it's because you stopped questioning it and became convinced that it's true. As such, challenging your beliefs is the first step to overcoming them.

Start by picking one of your most prominent limiting beliefs. Now, imagine that your limiting belief is a table, and its four legs are some of your current assumptions.

Let's come back to the previous example about people who reneged on their promises. This belief would represent the table. The four legs (assumptions) could be:

People should do what they promise.

When someone says they'll help me, it means they're fully committed to doing so.

What I'm asking for is as important to them as it is to me.

People are 100% reliable and should never make mistakes.

Are these assumptions true? Is it possible that I misinterpreted things? Let's look at the assumptions one at a time to see whether they're correct. One way to do that is to consider the viewpoint of those who promised to help and try to think from their perspective.

What if it wasn't a real commitment to them?

What if they thought that what I asked them wasn't important at all? Sure, it's important to me, but they're probably busy and have other priorities.

What if they just forgot about it? After all, nobody is perfect.

Turning things around

Another strategy is to direct the questions to myself and see what I would do in a similar situation:

I should keep my promises - Yes. I believe I should, but it doesn't mean I'm 100% reliable. I wish it did, but that's not the case.

I'm 100% reliable and never make mistakes. - Of course not. As much as I would like this to be true, it isn't. I'm human, and sometimes I forget to do something, or I get lazy.

Looking for counterexamples

The next step is to look at specific examples where I didn't do what I said I would do. I can think of a lot of cases where I didn't deliver something on time or didn't follow through on a commitment.

Looking at the consequences of your belief

What are the effects of holding your limiting belief? How does it make you feel? How much suffering does it create in your life? Often, it's when you're sick and tired that you finally commit to making the necessary changes in your life. Eliciting strong negative emotions will help you create new empowering beliefs and get rid of the old ones. The angrier you get about having bought into that stupid belief your whole life, the better you'll be able to overcome it and replace it with a new, empowering one. Doesn't it piss you off to have a belief that has been holding you back for so many years? It should! Take a moment to think of how your belief has been holding you back. Now, do you want to continue living your life this way? Do you want to allow this thought to control all areas of your life? Or do want you want to take control of what you believe and start changing your life?

Envisioning who you would be without that belief

Now, imagine if you could use a magic wand to remove that belief entirely. How would that make you feel? What kind of person would you be without that belief?

Remember that a belief is like a costume you wear. It's an identity you give to yourself. If you don't like what you're wearing, you can change it. That's one of the incredible powers of the human mind. You can plant new seeds (thoughts) in it at any time. These new seeds will give birth to a new tree (belief) that will bear fruit (results obtained by the actions you took based on what you now believe).

Coming up with a new, empowering belief

Limiting beliefs are like bad habits; they don't disappear on their own. They have to be replaced by something better. Once you identify a limiting belief, you want to substitute it for a new, empowering one. Look at your limiting belief and ask yourself, what would be the opposite of that?

For instance:

I don't have the time to start a business → I find and make time for whatever I'm committed to.

I'm not smart enough → I'm as capable as anyone else and I can always learn more, grow, and improve.

I'm not confident → I can sometimes lack confidence, but I can also be very self-confident depending on the situation.

Validating your new empowering belief

The next step is to strengthen your new belief. One way to do that is by looking at examples that prove it.

It could be:

Role models or people who show that your new, empowering belief is justified.

Past examples in your personal life that show your new belief is correct.

Let's say your new belief is "I find and make time for whatever I'm committed to." You might look online for people who successfully created a business despite a hectic schedule and lots of personal responsibilities.

You might also want to look at people to whom you can easily relate. If you're a single mom who wants to start an online business, for instance, look for other single moms who created successful businesses. If you search hard enough, I'm pretty sure you'll find single moms with multiple children who managed to build successful companies. So why not you?

The more you look at examples that validate your new, empowering belief, the more you'll realize that most of your limiting beliefs are false. Do you think you're too old to run a marathon? Well, the oldest person to finish a marathon was over 100. Do you think you're too shy or lack confidence and that you'll never be able to overcome it? You'll find people who were extremely shy and become insanely confident. If they can do it, why can't you?

I like to believe that other people are no smarter than me. If they can do it, I can do it, too. I highly encourage you to adopt a similar belief.

Another way to validate your new, empowering belief is to look at past examples from your own life. If you believe that you don't have time to start a business, can you think of a time in the past when you were overwhelmingly busy but managed to achieve your goals due to your commitment to them? These could be relationship goals, financial goals, health goals, *etc.* If so, can't you find and make the time for a new commitment?

Do you believe you lack confidence? Well, aren't there areas in your life in which you feel confident? Maybe you feel confident when you play sports. Or perhaps it's when you cook. You don't lack confidence. You already have confidence; you just need to spread it out to more areas in your life. Or maybe there was a time in the past when you felt confident. What were you doing? Why were you feeling that way?

Final tip

Remember that your mind likes to generalize things. That's why we hold so many stereotypes. To be able to understand the world, our brain needs to label things and classify them. The same goes for your beliefs. Your beliefs are generalizations that do not accurately reflect reality. They don't need to, but you want them to serve you, not to work against you.

What if you replace "I've never had confidence" with "There are situations in which I lack confidence, but there are also situations in which I feel confident"?

As for the third belief, is it true that you aren't good at anything? Not one, single thing? I doubt it. You could replace that statement with "There are things I'm not good at, but there are also things I do well." Don't forget that you can always grow and learn. We all have thousands of things we suck at, and that's perfectly normal. There's nothing to be ashamed of here.

The bottom-line is this: You don't need to get overly attached to your limiting beliefs. They aren't nearly as real as you think they are.

CHAPTER 6:

Integrating your new beliefs

Installing New Success Beliefs

You were not born with some other beliefs; you developed and acquired them all over time. As a consequence, you may alter an older belief or obtain a new one in the event you select. This doesn't suggest you could merely challenge the impression, and you will be dwelling.

The famous aphorism "Nature abhors a vacuum" is remarkably accurate in your mind. If you remove an older opinion, it creates a void that begs to be stuffed.

That is why you have to select and put in a brand-new belief to take the place of this older one. Imagine you could visit the shop and get any notion you desired, as though it were a bit of software, which you can take home and put in on your PC.

You can, metaphorically speaking.

That computer is the mind, and it is ready and waiting to take any new applications you select. So, ask yourself what beliefs could be useful for you to install on your computer.

Vital Success Attitudes and Beliefs which make Change Possible

There is a larger picture, but that is a greater priority for you at this stage. What could happen if you thought nothing worked for you or you weren't able to shed weight? Imagine if you believed it'd be great to slim down; however, it was not that important for you right now? Imagine if you're indifferent? These kinds of negative attitudes and beliefs could override and undermine all others under them. That is why the ideal approach to begin bettering your mind is to concentrate on the higher-level beliefs and think about them the essentials or requirements for your own success. These are the beliefs that make change possible.

Possibility: It is Achievable

As you have to open yourself to doubt that your old limiting beliefs, so you need to open yourself to think your new aims are possible.

Capability: I'm Able

The possibility is if you think something could be accomplished. Ability is when you think something could be done by you. Finding role models is a highly effective tool for altering beliefs, but in a few instances, it is insufficient.

To assist boost belief in yourself, first, research your previous experience. Consider a time when you had a target; you did not think it was possible. However, you attained it anyhow. It may be an academic or intellectual accomplishment. It may be in athletics. It may be a creative undertaking.

It may be a thriving connection. Even though it had been far removed from wellness or physical fitness objectives, it is evidence that you've got the capability to attain things you thought you were not capable of accomplishing. Secondly, start to collect new signs by taking action in your exercise program and beginning to collect modest successes.

Maintain your large goals in your mind, but place lots of short-term aims too. Pick simple things you are convinced you can readily achieve.

Necessity: I Have to Attain It

Possibility signifies you think it could be accomplished. Ability means you think it can be achieved by you. Necessity means you have to take action now or else. People will typically remain the same before the pain of remaining the exact same becomes greater than the pain of shifting. When you are dissatisfied, finally, that atmosphere builds up until it reaches a threshold.

Worthiness I Deserve It

Many individuals are unsatisfied with their own bodies. That is perfectly ordinary. The need to better one's situation is hardwired to each human being. But not confuse the urge for advancement together with the belief that you are not good enough the way you're. The issue is, disliking your body is able to become disliking yourself. Disliking yourself turns into reduced self-worth, so you think you do not deserve good things in life, such as a lean and healthy body. Low self-worth readily contributes to apathy, depression, or self-sabotage.

Desire: I Need It

After you state, "I need this," it is a statement of appetite. How badly you need something is dependent upon how important it's to you.

Everything on the significant list on your life is referred to as a value and worth are among the most effective beliefs. You literally arrange your whole life around them.

What is most and least significant for you influences the way you invest your time and sets the boundaries and criteria for your behaviors.

Expectation: I Expect It

Physicians and psychologists state that expectancy is the energy behind the placebo effect. In case a suffering person is given a sugar pill, and a respected physician congruently advises them that it is a powerful new painkiller, the individual becomes instant relief, even if the tablet has been an inert chemical.

Willingness: I'm Willing

Ultimately, your success is going to be a measure of just how prepared you are to do exactly what it requires. Personal development programs promising to help you accomplish your goals have become part of popular culture now, and I feel that is a fantastic thing. We can replicate our learning curve by discovering and learning from tutors. Alas, the urge to get

Exercise: Changing Beliefs

Pick a quiet spot to sit down by yourself. Then think of one belief that you want to get rid of. Once you've done that take out a pen and paper or use your computer. Start thinking the thoughts that you have that act in accordance to this belief. Once you've got your thoughts down on paper, then start thinking how they could have originated. Remember your childhood, times that made you sad, friends, and acquaintances. Anything and anyone that could have installed this belief in you. Write every single occurrence that could have been the cause of that belief down. Then pick one and work with it the day you are doing the exercise. For the next day you are going to work with the next one. Until that belief is no more. Pick one and try to remember the exact moment that this occurrence happened. Try to hear what you heard, see what you saw, and feel how you felt. If you parents told you something, then just make changes to what you thought was true back then. Reframe your thoughts and experience on the dialogue with your parents. If they said something like "You can never do anything right" change the meaning. Just think "I have done plenty of things right." Or "Mom just had a bad day. She didn't mean it" Then find evidence for why that belief is false and write it down. You are done for the day. If you are feeling the feelings you felt when this occurrence happened, you're doing it right. The next day pick the next occurrence and work with it. After you've destroyed this belief choose a new one and start over.

CHAPTER 7:

Building fundamental beliefs

The power of beliefs

One of the biggest lies we humans choose to accept is that our beliefs are facts. We all want to think our opinions, convictions and views accurately reflect reality. That what we believe in is true. No one likes to be wrong. Our beliefs greatly influence our emotions and actions, and we use them to understand and navigate the world. Many researchers would agree that the majority or our core and fundamental beliefs are formed by the age of six. Generally, these beliefs are formed in two ways: through our own experiences and by accepting what others tell us to be true. Once formed, our beliefs become embedded in us. And they play a critical role in shaping the direction of our lives. Regardless of whether they are actually true or not, we live as if they are factual. Our beliefs determine if we consider something to be good or bad, right or wrong, beautiful or ugly, safe or dangerous, or acceptable or unacceptable. Beliefs influence our decisions—whether we choose to follow our dreams or accept mediocrity, complain or take action, hit the gym or spend the evening on the couch. Beliefs matter. But how can we give so much credit to something that by its very definition is not a fact? If we look at the dictionary definition, nowhere will you find the word "fact." Instead, it is defined as:

An acceptance that a statement is true or that something exists. A firmly held opinion or conviction.

Even if multiple people agree on it, a belief is only a thought in the mind that we have thought long enough to the point where we accept it as true. There is no need to be attached to any of them or be convinced they are truth. We don't even need to accept them, especially those that don't serve us. You are as capable as you want to be. You are as worthy as you think.

So often we pass up potential opportunities because we allow the mind to tell us we "can't." This is your conscious mind operating on fears developed from past experiences and other people's belief systems. Once an idea or a thought enters your mind, you only have a few seconds to act on it before the conscious mind talks you out of it with excuses like: *I can't afford it, I'm not smart enough, the industry has too much competition and so on. Before you know it, the idea is out of reach, according to your mind.*

The great news is, it's completely in your control and you need ZERO resources to change the thoughts you choose to think. Ignore your conscious mind (the one you can hear) to tap into your subconscious mind (the creative workspace that is constantly drowned out by all the noise) by practicing silence. Stop concerning yourself with all the details. Take some sort of action to get you going immediately, and the answers you need will come when you need them. Your subconscious mind already has all the answers. You just need to believe in yourself and the possibilities.

Do your labels define you?

We often identify with labels to describe who we are. Unfortunately, in many cases these labels limit us. Labels categorize our personalities based on the work we do, our hobbies and our behaviors. We are not our labels, but often we choose to identify with them and believe they are true.

It is completely unnecessary to identify with any label, even if an event or circumstance has given you validity to do so. You are not your labels. Your soul is pure. It is, however, the mind that wants labels. Labels help our minds feel comfortable in an uncertain world. They help us feel like we "fit in" and justify our actions and experiences. With enough practice, you can teach your mind not to believe these labels by telling it what you *want* to identify with instead.

Regardless of what your beliefs are, the fact of the matter is that your beliefs are just that—beliefs, not facts. Understanding this can help you change your beliefs and achieve limitless potential.

We can challenge and change our beliefs as often as we desire because there is no need to get attached to them—they're just thoughts.

Do your actions support your beliefs?

We have so many beliefs, yet there are many of us who are not living the beliefs that they so strongly believe. For example, I've met a person who believes "all rich people are evil and selfish" and another who swears that "money changes people." You probably won't be surprised to learn that both these people were not financially fulfilled.

We compare ourselves to others. We remind ourselves of what we "can't" do or what is impossible. We create excuses and justify our arguments for not chasing our dreams.

Stop wasting precious moments, because of yours or others' beliefs: even if you think you can't, give it a go anyway. Find the way to believe you *can*. What other people think is none of your business.

Choose what you believe; change it if you need to (and as often as you like). Make sure your beliefs serve you and live what you believe.

Now it's your turn

Take the time to observe your beliefs. What do you fight for? What are your limitations and the boundaries you set for yourself? What are your beliefs about money, love, happiness and success?

Once you have identified the beliefs that shape your perspective, ask yourself, "How do I know whether my beliefs are true? What evidence do I have to prove their accuracy? Do they support my dreams or hold me back? If they are of no benefit to you, stop believing them. Think the thoughts that propel you towards your best life, and eventually those will not only start to dominate your mind but materialize in your real life.

Changing your own beliefs is easier than you may think. Identify a limiting belief that holds you back in life, then go to Google and research the opposite. You'll almost certainly find many facts and arguments that discredit what you think.

CHAPTER 8:

How your Own mind works

Subconscious Beliefs

The human mind can be divided into the conscious mind and the subconscious mind. The subconscious mind is more powerful than the conscious mind, so it can make someone to think, feel, and behave in a certain way without him knowing it. What is inside your subconscious mind can influence you when taking decisions and actions. The subconscious mind can either support you or hinder you in achieving your dream. So, what's you put in your subconscious mind determines your life achievement.

You may have heard it many times that the influence of the subconscious mind in one person's behavior is 88%, while the conscious mind influences the remaining 12%. But the newest research has proven that the subconscious mind is responsible for 95% to 99%, and determines almost all decisions, actions, emotions, and behaviors of one person. In other words, the subconscious mind is 99 times more powerful than the conscious mind.

The subconscious mind is controlling our lives. You might think, "How is it possible? I live consciously. I couldn't be controlled by my subconscious mind!" Are you sure? The subconscious mind is the center of memories, emotions, habits, perceptions, creativities, beliefs, values, personalities, *etc.* Can you live without them? No, you can't. Well, you are indeed live consciously, but the subconscious mind can influence or control you without you knowing it. The subconscious mind dominates your life more than you can imagine.

How does the subconscious mind influence your decisions and actions? There is a force within you that can drive you to pursue or avoid something, the force is emotions.

All this time, we are taught that by controlling our thoughts, we can control our feelings. Positive thought creates positive feeling, positive feeling creates positive behavior, and positive behavior creates positive result. But in fact, it's not that easy. As I mentioned before, when someone is controlled or ruled by his emotion, he will have little or no ability to think rationally. When someone feels negative, it is very difficult or almost impossible to think positive. Basically, thoughts can't win against emotions. When there is a conflict between the conscious and the subconscious mind, the subconscious mind will win. When there is a conflict between thoughts and emotions, emotions will win.

One thing you need to note is don't force yourself to think positive, especially when you are feeling negative! Many books always advise you think positive when you feel negative. For example, you set a goal, but you feel uncomfortable and negative self-talk appears, "I can't achieve it." Most books advise you to change the negative self-talk into positive thoughts, "No! It is not true! I can achieve it! Believe in yourself! Yes, I can achieve it!" Well, don't ever do this! Because this is an act of self-destruct.

Human memories are holographic, so they have an ability to cross-reference. There is no stand-alone memory. I believe you have often experienced it many times. Have you ever thought something and end up thinking something else? Maybe you thought of your income, and then you thought about your company, then the traffic jam, then a car, then your cousin, and so on. From one thought to another thought. One memory is associated with another memory. Everything is interrelated.

The same thing happens when you feel negative and try to think positive. Do you know that it will trigger negative memories in the subconscious mind? In this context, the more you try to be positive, the more negative you become. This is rarely recognized and understood by most people. I have often met people who become stress because of positive thinking.

When you feel negative and trying to think positive, you actually suppress your negative emotion. The negative emotions don't go anywhere, it is still in your subconscious mind. If you let it reside in there too long, it will become an illness, stress, and in the worst cases, suicide.

When you feel negative, positive thinking is only worsening your condition. To get the benefits of positive thinking, you first need to feel positive!

Your thoughts are in charge of your behaviors. But if your emotions rule or dominate you, emotions will beat thoughts and take over your behaviors. When you are ruled by your emotions, it is hard to think rationally, that's when your emotion takes over your behavior. Your emotion takes over your behavior and you will behave according to your emotion.

The most obvious example is a phobia. If you have a phobia, when you see or feel what you fear, you will end up being fear without being able to analyze whether it is scary or not. When the fear dominates you, you will behave according to it, you will run, scream, or faint.

So where does emotion come from? An emotion appears or is triggered because of a certain stimulus. When you get a certain stimulus, the stimulus will then activate a certain memory in your subconscious mind, the memory will then bring a certain emotion. For example, a song. When you hear a certain song, it makes you to remember a certain moment in your life, and it will make you to feel happy, sad, excited, *etc.*

A stimulus will also activate your belief system. Beliefs are what you believe to be true. And belief system is a set of or a group of beliefs that create a system and influence how you think, feel, and behave. What if you think, feel, and behave in a certain way? Obviously, you will achieve a certain result. But what if the result is not what you want? Then you have to change your belief. But changing belief at the conscious level is not enough, you have to change your belief in the subconscious mind! Change your subconscious belief, change your life!

Beliefs are called as beliefs because they are just beliefs, not facts. Beliefs are just ideas or opinions and not based on facts. But these ideas influence someone to think, feel, and behave according to it. Basically, humans don't react to the reality. They react to the internal reality in their heads. For example, person A believes that person B is a bad guy. Anything person B does, person A will think it as a bad thing. Even person B does a good thing in front of person A, person A will think that person B has a hidden purpose. Do you know a person who thinks negative towards another person like this?

Beliefs are just personal ideas or opinions. And beliefs are subjective. Let's use a phobia as the example again. Do you think a button is something scary? No! Which part of a button that is scary? But that is our opinions, but what about people who have a phobia of a button? For those who have a phobia of a button consider that a button is very scary. This belief, even it is not a fact, influences a person's thought, feeling, and behaviors. Those who fear of button would choose clothes that don't have any buttons. This is the case of a phobia, what if someone is programmed to fear of success?

If a person is programmed to be afraid of success, he will definitely stay away from success. A girl saw his parents were always fighting. When she watched a TV drama, she also saw unpleasant marriage life story. When talking with her friend, her friend told her that their parents were always arguing. Then she believed that marriage life was unpleasant. As an adult, this belief hindered her in a relationship aspect, especially when she wanted to get married. Many men were attracted to her, but she always refused with unclear reasons. Consciously she wanted to have a partner and got married, but something hindered her. When dating, the belief triggered uncomfortable feelings and made her date failed. Unconsciously, this belief told her not to build a relationship with anyone, let alone to get married, because marriage life was unpleasant.

A belief is formed when we agree with the idea that we see, hear, and feel. The process of belief formation has begun even when we were still in our mother's womb. Most beliefs are formed when we were kids, when we were 0 until 13 years old, because at that time, our conscious minds were still not able to analyze incoming information critically. So, what we saw, heard, and felt went directly into the subconscious mind. And when we agree with the idea or incoming information, a belief is formed. The belief will attach to us until the rest of our lives.

For example, and this is always happening in our education world, a kid got a poor grade. The teacher then scolded him, "You stupid! Did not you study? Did you not pay attention when I explained this subject? You fool!" When the kid went home and showed the test result to his parents, his parents scolded him the same thing, "You stupid kid! How could you get a poor grade? What are you doing in school? Did you not study? Stupid kid! "

The information entered directly into the subconscious without filtered. Until here, the information was no more than an idea and only stopped at the short-term memory folder. But when the kid agreed with the idea, "I am stupid. I always get bad grades. My parents and teachers are right. I am a stupid kid." When the kid agreed with the idea, a belief was formed. The kid definitely became a stupid kid. Not because he was stupid, but because the suggestion that was given by his parents and teacher.

Beliefs can be divided into two, empowering beliefs and limiting beliefs. Empowering beliefs are beliefs that support your achievement, while limiting beliefs are beliefs that hinder your achievement.

When you believe something, you will behave congruently with that belief. If you behave in a certain way, you will get a certain result. If you believe you can do it, then you can do it. But if you believe you can't do it, then you can't do it. That is why subconscious beliefs are often called self-fulfilling prophecy.

If you an empowering belief, you can achieve your dream quickly and your life will be easy.

What if you have a limiting belief? A limiting belief will always hinder you. Don't underestimate beliefs. Beliefs are not visible, but it can influence you more than you can imagine. Your beliefs determine your success in every aspect. If beliefs determine your success, then you have to develop empowering beliefs and remove limiting beliefs.

One the characteristics of the human mind is seeking pleasure and avoiding pain. Pain and pleasure, carrot and stick, reward and punishment, or whatever you want to call it. Pain and pleasure are the best approach to make the subconscious mind to change. By using pain and pleasure, we tell the subconscious mind that there are consequences if it keeps holding a limiting belief.

For example, money. Most people have a wrong interpretation about money. Let's say you believe that money is the root of evil. If you believe that money is the root of evil, your mind will avoid having a lot of money. Your mind will sabotage all the thoughts, feelings, and behaviors that are related to things that can make you earn more money. This is why you often hear about people who become rich instantaneously by winning a lottery, but immediately lost their wealth and become poorer. They had a limiting belief about money. If they don't remove their limiting beliefs, even they won lotteries a thousand times, they will keep losing their money.

The reason we keep holding our limiting beliefs is because we believe that we can feel pleasure and avoid pain if we keep holding it. So if we tell our subconscious minds that we can feel more pleasures once we remove our limiting beliefs and feel more pain if we keep holding it, the subconscious mind will be likely to remove our limiting beliefs.

By using the techniques called The Dickens Process, we can tell our subconscious minds what the consequences if we keep holding our limiting beliefs. The Dickens Process is an NLP technique popularized by Anthony Robbins in his *Unleash the Power Within* Seminar. This NLP pattern is based upon the Charles Dickens' character. Scrooge meets the Ghost of Christmas Future and he was shown what would happen to him in the future if he kept up his current behavior.

Before we practice the Dickens Process, answer the following questions:

- How long have you held this limiting belief?

- What are the qualities of your life all this time?

- What are bad things you have experienced because of this limiting belief?

- What are bad things you will experience if you keep holding this limiting belief?

- Imagine and feel all the bad things that you have experienced because of this limiting belief!

- Decide earnestly and sincerely to release this limiting belief!

- What are 5 benefits you will get after removing this limiting belief?

- Imagine and feel all the benefits you will get when you remove this limiting belief!

After you done answering the questions, your limiting beliefs will begin to shake. Next is using the Dickens Process to remove your limiting beliefs completely:

1. Imagine yourself go 5, 10, and 20 years into the future. Imagine what it would be like if you have not changed yourself. What are the consequences if you keep staying as the way you are now?

2. Wake up from this bad dream. It is morning and none of those things have happened yet. Drink a water to calm yourself first. Believe to yourself that you still have the opportunity to change everything.

3. Imagine yourself go 5, 10, and 20 years into the future. Imagine what it would be like if you have changed yourself. Associate with the massive pleasure! What it would be like if you had changed yourself? What it would feel like after you had changed yourself?

You need to keep in mind that pain and pleasure can't be separated or used alone. If we are focused on the pain, we often create more pain. After associating your limiting beliefs with massive pain, immediately associate it with massive pleasure.

In order for this technique to work, you have to go into a trance state or a hypnotic state. Most people fail to get the benefits from this technique is because they practice it in a conscious state, so only their conscious minds that aware of the pain and pleasure, while their subconscious minds don't know or realize it. So, you need to go into a hypnotic state before practicing this technique.

CHAPTER 9:

How to get the results you want

How to Break Through

When you understand that a breakdown *always* occurs prior to a breakthrough, you can begin to turn the situation around. Not only does your perspective change, but your response changes, as well. Instead of losing confidence, you begin to view the setback as just one more hurdle on your way to growing a successful business. Take a moment and consider that. When you begin to train your mindset to switch from focusing on the problem to discovering solutions, your response changes. Instead of viewing situations as barriers, you view them as challenges to overcome. There is nothing like a good challenge to spark a growth-minded entrepreneur's desire to excel.

Too often, however, a breakdown will stop entrepreneurs because they are too identified with their egos. When I refer to the ego, I mean the part of us whose primary job is to keep us safe. Unfortunately, the ego tries to keep us safe by preventing us from actually taking risks and pushing ourselves. It can't discriminate between positive risk and negative risk and views all risk as unsafe.

The doubts, fears, and worries you experience are created by the ego as it attempts to keep you where you are. Its perspective appears very, very real. It is the source of your resistance.

Among other things, your ego is concerned with your image and how other people perceive you, external factors you are unable to control. Your ego is highly judgmental.

The more you move past your doubts and fear and continue to push yourself despite them, the less you are in need of your ego—and the last thing the ego wants is extinction, so it raises the alarm even more. How? By causing you to experience more doubt and by bringing in guilt and shame.

Rather than trying to extinguish the ego and thus setting the stage for an internal battle to the death, aim instead for transformation. Become aware of your thoughts and emotions, and then change your response. Instead of believing you have to "do" something because you are feeling a certain way, just observe your emotions. See if you can acknowledge or name what you are feeling. You are much more complex than happy, sad, bored, or angry. You don't need to do anything else. You don't have to try to change the feeling. Eventually, it will change on its own.

I know this seems counterintuitive because we are so conditioned to respond but give it a try for one week and see how it is to note your emotions, whether fear, doubt, or worry, and to not act on them. The choice is yours: act or react.

How to Transform the Ego Response

If you tend to be skeptical and are always on the lookout for when you are going to get scammed, your distrustfulness and doubts may stop you from taking action. However, those same qualities also mean you are able to see down the road, to see the big picture. You are a strategist. The work, then, is to use those qualities in a positive way instead of letting them stop you.

In truth, a setback or a breakdown is only a test of your commitment to your vision. View them as challenges and reconnect to your Big Why. Remember your motivation for being a successful entrepreneur in the first place.

When you view setbacks as challenges, they don't knock you down. You just find a new way forward. You emerge victorious.

How Do You See the World?

Your life is like a movie, and the person sitting next to you or in the other room is viewing a very different movie. The director of your movie is your perception. The way you experience anything, and everything comes from how you perceive it. Is a setback a challenge or a catastrophe? It depends on how you view it. The way you view a setback is determined by your experiences, the meanings you ascribed to them, and the beliefs you created from them.

What if setbacks are only illusions, similar to the distractions that occur when people compete? Not only can you change the way you view setbacks, but you can also change the lens of your perception. You can change the way you see *anything*. We are going to start with beliefs.

Beliefs Are Not Always Based on Logic

Beliefs are powerful. They determine whether or not you are going to be a go-getter. Consider the unknowns who became exceptional industry leaders despite the odds against them. They believed they were capable of great results, and they were. However, there are many more entrepreneurs who possessed the technical ability to make an impact but didn't believe they were capable. Their stories are rarely told.

Basically, a belief is the relationship between a thought and an emotion. As we grow up, situations and people influence us. Things happen in our lives that have emotional impacts. We create meanings around them and then form beliefs based on those meanings.

There is a difference between belief and reality. Beliefs are not always based on facts or logic, although they can feel very true. Beliefs, however, shape your reality.

Subconscious beliefs are always more powerful than conscious beliefs, in part because they operate under the surface and we usually don't know they are there—but they still direct our actions.

In fact, if you have two opposing beliefs, one conscious and the other subconscious, the subconscious belief will always dominate.

Conscious and subconscious beliefs are often in opposition to one another. Many subconscious beliefs are based on situations that don't exist anymore, and they were usually founded on incomplete information to begin with.

Two opposing beliefs, especially a conscious and a subconscious belief, create conflict and an inner struggle. For example, you might say you are committed to be a successful business owner, but if you subconsciously believe you don't deserve it or don't want the attention, you will hold yourself back, or worse yet, sabotage your success. Or you may become a perfectionist, slowing down your progress to avoid being judged for making a mistake.

Inner struggles are draining. Trying to think them through or tough them out will not help, because the struggle is not based on logic. It is energetic. It is like a water hose with a kink in it. No matter how far you turn the faucet, the water will not flow. The kink holds back the water, creating pressure in the hose. Once you take the kink out, the water flows freely.

When you develop an inner struggle because of two opposing beliefs, your energy has a kink in it, and progress becomes very difficult. Clear the kink, and you begin to progress once more.

How to Clear the Kink

Some beliefs are easily changed on your own once you recognize them. Others are more challenging. They can be changed but are more deeply rooted. Once you are genuinely ready to replace your beliefs with something new and relevant, it will happen. Change is possible.

To begin to clear your own kink caused by conflicting beliefs, try the same three-prong approach:

Uncover the hidden beliefs affecting your actions

First, examine your resistance. Where are you not excelling as expected? When do you hold yourself back? When do you make excuses, blame others, or feel fear? In those situations, you are likely experiencing conflicting beliefs. Choose one situation and try to find the belief that is informing your action or inaction. (To do this, you might need the assistance of a therapist or business coach.)

Discover the relationship between the belief and the consequences it is having on your actions

The easiest way to do this is to become aware of the thoughts you have as you are doing different activities. How do those thoughts influence your actions? After you complete a specific activity, write down where you experienced flow and what was occurring. Also note when you felt that remaining focused was difficult and what was going on then.

Regain control by exploring alternative beliefs better suited for your current reality, and put those beliefs into action

The ideal time to do this is at the end of the day, when you have time to reflect on your activities.

If you have difficulty with this exercise, don't despair. Sometimes, it takes a trained professional to help you clear the obstacles to success. As it is with mentoring, transforming the obstacles will occur at a faster pace when you work with someone else than when you work on them on your own.

The Power of Your Story

The beliefs you have feel true, but they are creations of your experiences. They stem from your interpretations of the things that happen to you and the stories you tell yourself in order to make sense of the events. We all have a story, and each of our stories is unique. Our stories can inspire us or hold us back. You will learn how even the ones that hold you back can be transformed.

Retool Your Inner Critic

A relentless inner critic can cause a kink that prevents you from thinking like a leader. Most top entrepreneurs have very high standards for themselves. They feel they never perform to their best capabilities, that there is always something they could do to push their limit a bit more. Those thoughts of always wanting to do more and never being satisfied can, and do, motivate a person to try harder and to work harder.

At a certain point, however, self-criticism can backfire. Those thoughts of never doing well enough are very negative, and negativity slows down progress. For instance, when you are critical of yourself, you tend to second-guess everything you do, causing you to hold back, fearful of making a mistake and being criticized again, if only by yourself. And giving so much energy to what you are not doing well drains you. It is exhausting.

Change is difficult when you are focused on what you don't want to do, what is not working for you, and what you are not doing well. When you keep looking behind you, you are going against the flow and hindering your success. Remember, whatever you focus on expands.

When you think negative thoughts, you will always find evidence to support your reality. It is like rafting upstream on a river. By going against the current, you spend a lot of energy resisting the river's natural flow. It is tiring and exhausting. For the amount of effort, you are exerting, you have little gain in return. On the other hand, when you turn your raft around to go downstream with the natural current of the river, it flows easily with little effort.

In the same way, when you turn your attention toward what *is* working, what you *are* doing well, and where your business is improving, you are looking forward. You are positive and hopeful, excited by what is possible. Your raft is now going downstream, aided by the current. You begin taking steps toward reaching your full potential.

It is important, however, to be aware of the messages your critical voice is telling you. If you are not aware of them, you cannot change the situation. Some entrepreneurs are not aware, so they are attacked and don't even know it. As a result, they may act out, underachieve, or be unpredictable or moody.

How to Become Aware of the Inner Critic

If you are not aware of the self-critical voice in your head, it is possible to learn to hear it. Just as you keep records on your business cash flow, you can keep a log or journal on the thoughts you have that create distraction for you. You can also keep a log of thoughts that create laser focus. You might be surprised to find that when you are laser focused, your mind is clear and free of all thought. When you begin to log your thoughts, you start to bring something that was subconscious up to the surface. Once you are aware of those hidden thoughts, you can begin to change the situation.

Next, it is important to understand how those negative thoughts affect your performance. As you are writing in your log, record the connections between thoughts and a specific result. For instance, you are a graphic designer, and you recall that you were beating yourself up for taking an unexpected call while working on a project that was due the next day and, as a result, you lost focus. This is the connection between the thought (beating yourself up) and its result (losing focus).

Once you become aware of the self-critical messages, the trick is not to believe them. They sound justified, but they are not. They originally came from someone else, perhaps a parent or teacher. Most likely you heard them from someone you wanted praise from but never got. You can choose to transform your inner critic, and as you do, you are freeing yourself of the negative drag on your actions.

An Exercise to Sidestep Your Inner Critic

Here are six steps for transforming your relationship with the inner critic:

1. First, understand that the inner critic is fearful. Fearful thoughts can easily take on a life of their own, causing a complete halt of any progress if ignored. What are the fears that keep you stuck?

2. You get to choose how you view your progress and performance. Despite what your inner critic says, you don't have to focus on the negative, on what you are not doing well, in order to excel. Remember, to do so is like rafting upstream. Create a strengths-based approach, finding the positive activities that help you improve.

3. You may feel as though the inner critic is part of you, but it is not. Being aware of this will help you separate from the critical voice.

Where did the critical thoughts originate? If you hear them, do you recognize the voice?

4. Once you recognize you have a choice to release the inner critic, you have created your opportunity for change. Choose not to believe the voice anymore.

5. Your goal is not to annihilate the voice; your goal is to make it irrelevant. Do that by shifting your focus to the positive. Acknowledge the activities you are doing well. Become aware of your strengths. Choose the next step toward your vision. Think about your goals.

6. Notice the results. As you begin changing your perception and thinking like a growth-minded entrepreneur, the resistance to your excellence collapses, and you will start to see improvement in your actions. In addition, you will have a much-improved state of mind.

To be a successful entrepreneur, you have to think like a successful entrepreneur, see yourself as a successful entrepreneur, and act like a successful entrepreneur. Each of these steps is more involved than it seems on the surface.

You can choose to release yourself from the struggle, your resistance, and your inner critic. Thinking like a successful entrepreneur changes your brain chemistry and sets the stage for an upward spiral and a breakthrough in your actions. I know that is what you want, so let's continue.

How your subconscious removes mental blocks

Identify the core issue

Pick a Pattern

We all have destructive patterns. Even the most "together" of people have their weaknesses. Surely you know at least one thin, beautiful, successful woman who always dates the wrong guy. Maybe you've met the spiritual leader with the addiction to chocolate (or soda, or candy, or cigarettes), or the average man whose life works well—except that he turns into the Hulk and flips out if anyone questions his integrity.

When you're the one repeating the pattern, it can be hard to spot, at least until you become ready to shift it. And heaven help the friend or counselor who points it out to you with irrefutable evidence *before* you are ready to release it! Your inner Hulk will surely devour that poor soul.

Clear the Underlying Block

You might be surprised to learn that there are as many methods for clearing as there are people who are interested in clearing. Well, maybe not quite that many, but there are a crapload for sure, along with the ongoing development and discovery of new methods, as well as enhancements of old methods.

Need a thought-break? Take a few minutes to chew through some of the thoughts and feelings rattling around your head and heart. When you're ready to try on the possibility that you are God, then pick up this book again and continue as we dive into a trio of powerful clearing methods. Enjoy the pause, but don't wait too long, because I know you have some crap to clear and you'd like to get that handled sooner rather than later.

Cord Cutting

It's difficult to find information about the origin of cord cutting, most likely because there are so many variations of the process and it's been around for so very long. It's likely that the practice is based on the clipping of the umbilical cord between mother and child.

Permanent cord cutting in three easy steps:

Step 1: Visualize the setup

Step 2: Cut the cord

Step 3: Let it go

As you can see, cord cutting doesn't always have to be with a person. It could be with the amazing job you didn't get, the house you didn't qualify for, the money you lost in that bad investment, the one who got away, or even the book you've decided not to write after all.

It's about release, not revenge.

When we cut cords, we release all that no longer serves, with the highest and best intention for all involved.

Never cut cords from a place of spite or anger. If you cannot cut the cords with love, then you must at the very least be neutral about it; otherwise, you will find yourself right back where you started, as though the cord cutting never happened. Remember the weeds that got cut at ground level? They're back in no time, unlike the weeds that were completely removed, down to the roots.

Visualize the setup

Begin by imagining you are standing face to face with the person or thing you wish to release. Usually about two to four feet apart is sufficient. Next, visualize the cords that connect the two of you. Notice the cords and where they are attached. It is not necessary to interpret or analyze this, but simply to notice. In some cases, there are multiple cords running to and from different locations. There is no right answer here, so whatever you see is perfect. You don't need to write it down or judge what you see, but simply notice what pops into your awareness as you stand before the person or thing.

Next, is there anything you'd like to say before you cut the cord? Often there's nothing to say, while other times it's something like "I forgive you" or "I release you and ask that you release me" or "thank you and good-bye" or "I wish you well." If there's something you want to say, say it now. This helps to create a permanent release with complete closure.

The last step in the setup is to choose a tool, any tool you want. Keep in mind that we want to cut the cords in one fell swoop, so don't pick a hacksaw, a nail file, or anything that is going to require multiple strokes to sever.

The key to remember is when you cut, make one clean and swift cut. You don't want to be sawing or hacking away like you're a lumberjack. This is to be done in one fell swoop, and if you've got cords running every which way between you and what/whomever we're cutting cords with, then gather them all up into your hand before you raise your tool, so that you can get everything in one slice or snip or whack, depending on your tool of choice.

This next part is essential in making a cord-cutting permanent. When you cut, imagine that the cords (especially the part that runs between your body and the point where you cut) either disappear entirely, or fall to the ground and then disappear.

Let it go

The last step is symbolic of total and permanent release, and if you see something fishy here, then it's a good indication that you weren't completely neutral when you cut the cord. Once you cut the cords and see them fall away and disappear, watch the person (or thing) across from you float up and away from you, like a helium balloon set free. Watch until he/she/it shrinks away to just a speck, then disappears entirely. Incidentally, most people see the person or thing rise up and to the left, but that's not a hard-and-fast rule. When it's completely gone, you are done.

If you see something different happening, there may be more to do to complete this cord cutting, or it could be that you weren't entirely ready to release. One example of this would be if you cut the cords and they disappear, but the person won't go away, or they appear angry or hurt. Or they rise up into the air, but they're still tethered to you somehow. If this happens, do some more forgiveness work and then repeat the cord cutting later.

Occasionally, something unusual may happen when you cut the cord. The main thing to notice is how you feel at the end of the cord cutting. At the very least, you should feel neutral, and at the very best, you would experience a sense of peace or freedom. Some people sigh when the cord cutting is complete.

How can you tell if it's really, really, really finished?

Notice how you feel over the next few days. In many cases, the cord cutting is so thorough that you may forget you ever had an issue with this person or thing or circumstance. May sound crazy, but it's happened to me more than once. Incidentally, that's true of any kind of clearing, not just cord cuttings.

If it's incomplete, you will still have adverse feelings about the person or situation, or more likely, it will show up in your space before you even get to that tickler reminder.

In reality, the entire cord cutting process may take as little as a couple of minutes. But now that you understand the full process, and you know how to make it permanent, you are empowered to do your own permanent cord cutting.

Pack Your Bags, We're Taking a (Mental) Trip

Guided visualization is exactly what it sounds like, and the good news is that you don't need a guru or healing expert to walk you through it. You can actually create your own guided visualizations by simply opening your connection to Source and seeing what comes through.

A guided visualization for the purposes of clearing is a simple and effective way to release your blocks. Think of it as lucid dreaming. You create an imaginary scenario, an imaginary world (or one that's oddly familiar) and you walk yourself through a pleasant process that concludes with the release of your block, doubt, fear, or limiting belief.

Begin by taking a couple of deep breaths and getting settled and relaxed, right where you are. It's fine if you are sitting or lying down. I'm going to walk you through a very simple guided visualization exercise.

As you breathe and get comfortable, allow whatever you are sitting or lying on to support you fully. Just sink down into it. That's good.

Maybe you thought for a moment you wanted to strangle somebody or punch your fist through a wall. That would be a good example of what we're looking for here.

Have you got that time? I promise this will be the only unpleasant part; remembering this time when you were so angry.

As you recall that memory, notice what's lighting up inside your body. There will be one prominent spot in your body where this anger seems to flare. It could be in the front of your head. It could be in your throat – maybe you feel your throat closing now as it did then.

It could be in your chest, maybe you feel a tightness in your chest. It could be in the pit of your stomach. It could be someplace else entirely but notice the precise location where that anger appears to flare.

Turn your attention to the anger, to the location of it. The circumstances will start to fall away, but pay attention to the anger itself, and see if you can notice without judgment or analysis. For example, what characteristics does it have? Is it a certain color? Is it dense and dark and gray? Or is it fiery red, or is it white hot? I'm just giving you examples; there's no right answer here, and you don't have to recall any of this when we're done. Just be present with me in the moment, right now. Now you have a choice. On the one hand, you could keep the thing. You could reach out with your hand and stick it back in your body and continue to carry it with you.

Or, on the other hand, you could release it. You could let it go so that it will never be a part of you in this way again.

Make your decision now.

If you've decided to keep it, go ahead and place it back in your body and then just relax until the end of this visualization.

But if you've chosen to let it go, listen carefully because I will give you instructions. Right now, you should not be touching the object. It should be hovering just in front of you, and your hands are free. Here's what we are going to do: I'm going to count you down, "3-2-1 go," and when I say "go," you're going to put your hands around the object without touching it and you're going to encompass it in a big bubble, a bubble that is unbreakable by you. Then, when I say "push," you will push that bubble out and away from you. Then it will return to Source where it will be transformed into beautiful, perfect Light.

And if it is ever to return to you, it can only return to you in its perfect form (beautiful, perfect Light) that can only come to you as blessings and love.

Here we go, are you ready?

Three, two, one, go.

Without touching, shape your arms and your hands around the object and completely cover it in a bubble. Enclose it fully. When I say "push," you will push it out and away from you.

Three, two, one, push.

See it go? Way, way, way out, until it disappears! Tiny as a pinprick and then boom, it's gone.

Feel the freedom, the lightness, the weight that has been lifted. No longer are you carrying this particular burden of anger. And you can come back and repeat this exercise as other forms of anger are identified, and as you remember other betrayals and injustices from your past. The more anger you release, the lighter and freer you will feel. The more liberated you will be. Take a very deep breath and when you do, this time breathe in a sense of freedom and liberation, and then let it out slowly. As you let out this deep breath, you release tension from your body, tension you didn't even realize you were carrying all this time. Notice how you feel right now. Happy, free, peaceful, neutral?

You've done it! You've released this anger!

Know that when you are ready, you can return your awareness to your surroundings. You can stretch and open your eyes, but you don't have to. You can stay in this relaxed and peaceful space as long as you wish.

CHAPTER 10:

How to use your beliefs strategy to remove Fear

Fear is often considered by many in the self-help industry to be the enemy of success. Great rewards are obtained from taking risks in life. If fear often reigns within you, you'll never have the courage to take risks and you'd have a very difficult time accomplishing anything great.

Experiencing natural fear from time to time is part of life. It is a normal thing, but it can be physically and emotionally weakening if you live with constant fear. You won't be able to live your life to the fullest if you keep on refusing to join various daily activities just because you might have to face your fear of social interaction.

Even the bravest people in the world have certain fears that they have had to overcome. It doesn't really matter whether you're afraid of heights, spiders, failure, or change as long as you're courageous enough to accept, confront, and take control of your fears to keep them from restraining you, when it comes to the things you want to do most in your life.

Sooner or later, you may start to acquire new fears unconsciously, but you shouldn't dwell on them and make it a priority to unlearn those new fears as well. It's important not to deny having such fears and being aware of them is also essential, as you begin the first step towards eradicating them. Anyone can learn how to overcome fear. It's a skill. People usually just cling to them because their fears are a part of their entire disposition. There's nothing wrong if you feel like you're not yet ready to face your fears, but you will know when it is the right time. Once you've decided to start conquering your fears, here that the things that will help you accomplish your goals:

Analyze & Evaluate Your Fears

Acknowledge It

Ignoring or denying the fact that you have fears, even to yourself, is a very easy thing to do, especially when you want to appear brave or strong to others. The truth is, you can't really consider yourself as brave if you aren't able to accept the fact that you have fears in the first place.

Acknowledging your feelings is the first step in taking control over the situation. Write down on a sheet of paper, "I (insert name), am currently afraid of (insert fear) and I will overcome this fear because I want to accomplish….. "

Identify Your Fears

Sometimes fear can be easily recognized, but other times you can't even explain where those anxious feelings are coming from. Learn to name your fears. What is it exactly that makes you so afraid?

Once you understand what your fears are about, you're already on your way towards eliminating them.

Journaling can be a good way to keep track of your progress while you're striving to overcome your fears. Write down every fear that bothers you. Often times when I would write down the fears that I had, I started to realize that these fears only existed in my head and the chance of the occurrence actually happening in reality was slim to none.

Identify the Structure

Dealing with your fear and considering it as something that has a beginning and an end can surely help you realize that you have control over it. Delve into it's roots. When, where, and how did it begin? Did it start with a traumatic experience? Does it have anything to do with your childhood environment at school or home? How long have you been afraid of said thing? What triggers it and how does it affect you?

Fear is sometimes a healthy emotion that can protect you from harm or doing something silly. Find out whether you have a really good, realistic reason to possess this fear or if it is simply inhibiting.

Imagine Your Desired Outcome

As soon as you understand and recognize your fear, think about the things you want to change. Your main goal might be to overcome all of your limiting fears in life, but keep in mind that it is important to establish smaller, measurable goals to achieve success in the long-term.

Do it one step at a time. Imagine the person that you will be once you overcome the issues that you have right now and think about how beneficial it will be once you get there.

Take Charge of Your Fears

Gradually Lessen Sensitivity

Usually, people are afraid of things because they haven't correctly been exposed to them. We commonly describe it as "fear of the unknown". Try to expose yourself, little by little, to the things that you're afraid of, until you learn to understand them better and your fear of them will start to dissolve.

Try Direct Confrontation

Sometimes, the best way to overcome your fears is to confront them, face to face.

When you encounter the cause or basis of your fears, you might realize that there's really nothing to be afraid of and that you've just made up all those scary scenarios in your head. Imagination can make reality look terrifying if it gets out of control.

Once you've decided to take action, your fears become weaker and the new reality isn't as bad as you'd originally thought it would be.

Learn to Handle Failure

Facing your own fears can be quite difficult and challenging, and you don't always end up triumphant right away. You may have to face them many times before you can actually say that you've defeated your fears for good. You must make it a point to remember why you started on this journey in the first place.

Focus on how helpless you'll feel if you let the fear defeat you in the long run. This thought will help to drive you when times get tough. Remember that failure is only a stepping-stone on the road to your success. The world won't end when you fail at something, but your fear will stay scary if you quit and let it be that way for good.

Don't Stop the Momentum

Always remember that nothing is impossible when you're absolutely determined to achieve your goals. Perseverance is the key in getting past your fears. Don't worry about how much progress you made each day, just make sure that you are making progress over time. You should be trending upwards.

Let No One Stop You

There may be times when people will feed your fears and tell you that you're not good enough. Maybe they'll tell you that there's nothing you can do to change your current situation. Ignore these people and surround yourself with people who will boost your confidence and believe in your ability to overcome your challenges.

It is important to be open with others about what you are trying to overcome so that they can help you get through your struggles. It also helps to find someone who once feared what you currently fear and may have some strategies and tips that can be insightful for you.

Just as we mentioned earlier that negative influences can cause you to develop and maintain certain fears, the opposite is also true. You can influence yourself by listening, watching, and interacting with more positive people that encourage you. By doing so, you are stacking the odds in your favor and this is very important in regard to keeping your momentum going strong.

Change Your Perception About Fear

Turn Your Fear into Attraction

The things that allow us to feel fear stimulates feelings of excitement and passion as well, which is why there are people who love horror movies or engaging in extreme sports. Try re-assessing your fear on a positive note and learn to appreciate the joy and pleasure that it can offer you.

Once you make it as your source of energy, you might eventually welcome it into your life with open arms. Look at it as a challenge in your life that you are going to overcome, something that you will look back on in 5, 10, or 20 years from now and say "I did that!". This will help you to be more optimistic in your abilities when you are struggling.

Consider Fear as An Opportunity

Fear can be a way to help identify and solve problems effectively. It serves as a guide that tells us when certain aspects of our lives need attention. When something unfamiliar scares you, consider it as a sign that you might actually need to know someone or something better than you currently do.

When you fear an upcoming deadline, see to it that you turn it into an opportunity to prepare yourself, whether it's writing a paper or delivering a speech. If you have a fear of water, think about all the possibilities laid out in front of you as soon as you overcome your fear. The thought of riding a boat or swimming and having a good time with your friends can be a form of motivation. When fear gets into your nerves, simply think of some happy or positive thoughts.

Provide A Rightful Place for Fear in Your Life

Fear is a natural emotion just like joy and sadness. Being fearful can actually help build one's character and teaches us how to become brave. You don't need to push or force yourself to overcome a fear just because you notice one of the earlier signs. If you notice that you are nervous to drive 115 miles/hour on the freeway, you shouldn't look at it as a "challenge" and make it your mission to overcome it. Remember that if you notice a fear, any fear, come up in your life and you are wondering whether or not you should try to spend countless hours trying to overcome it, you can ask yourself an important question: "What kind of person will I become if I overcome this fear?" By answering this question, you will know if you should try to overcome it.

It is very important that you work on conquering the major obstacles in your life, but make sure that you don't strain yourself too much on things that don't result in any limitations to your daily life. The purpose of trying to overcome your fears is to free yourself to live a more positive life and to open up more doors of opportunity that you would not otherwise have.

Celebrate Your Triumphs

You don't have to wait until you've completely overcome your fear to celebrate. After you've set some small goals and made a few steps up that staircase, remember to reward yourself at every milestone you've hit. It could be something small, like when you saw a spider and didn't scream or travelled around the city all by yourself. When you realize and feel how good it is to conquer your fears, you're all set towards facing the next challenges in your life.

Seeking professional help is also a good way to overcome your fears, especially if your fears are affecting your personal happiness in multiple ways. A trained specialist can assist you in identifying the source of your fears and provide you with ways to cope with them. Sometimes people feel ashamed to see some type of therapist, but the real shame is living your whole life without taking any action. Don't ever feel ashamed if you are moving closer to your goals.

CHAPTER 11:

Aligning yourself with reality

Do you wish the world could be different with no wars or misery? I certainly do.

Unfortunately, the reality is that wars are occurring right now. And hundreds of millions of people live in misery. Now what if I tell you things are exactly the way they are, even though it's not the way you want them to be? But I hear you ask, "Thibaut, how can you be okay with the way the world is?"

People suffer and that is really unfortunate, but it also happens to be the truth. Reality simply *is*. And refusing to accept that as a fact is not only a sign of insanity, but also a sign of arrogance. It's like saying the world should be the way we picture it just because that's what *we* want.

Truth being said, reality can never be wrong. It has never been and never will be. How could what actually exists not exist?

Now, please bear with me. Understanding the concept that reality can't be wrong is critical because when we fail to acknowledge reality for what it is, we live in denial. And usually nothing constructive comes from living in denial.

Accepting reality as it is

The first step to achieving better results in any area of your life is to accept reality as it is. Put differently, we need to cultivate the most accurate model of reality possible. Because if your model is flawed, you'll take ineffective or even counter-productive action and will achieve mediocre results at best. In short, the best way to play the whole game of life is to align yourself with reality.

To "win" the game you need to know the rules—or at least have a solid understanding of what they are. This starts by accepting reality as it is, not by thinking it should be any different.

Should vs. is

There should be no poverty. All people should be treated equally. I should make more money. Have you ever thought along these lines?

The problem with believing things *should* be different is that it can put you in a disempowering state. It can also lead you to overlook reality and only live in an imaginary ideal world where everybody is happy and successful.

Now I'm not saying there is anything wrong with envisioning a better world. I'm all for it. However, before you do that, it is important you take a sincere and objective look at the reality in front of you. Ignoring reality will not help you take the appropriate action.

Should vs. could

A better way of thinking is to replace "should" with "could". While "should" implies that things aren't the way they're supposed to be, "could" offers possibilities, not judgment. You can choose to explore these possibilities, or you can reject them.

For instance, if you say, "I should be working", it implies that something is wrong with the current reality of you not working. You're emitting a judgment (i.e., you're lazy or undisciplined because you're not working). On the other hand, if you say, "I could be working", you accept the reality that you're not currently working. Then you're inviting yourself to work if you choose to. Can you see the difference between the two statements?

The point is, you can "should" yourself as much as you want, but it won't help. It will only lead you to feel guilty. Therefore, start noticing whenever you use the word "should". Then try using "could" instead and see how it makes you feel. Below are examples of the way our thinking can change based on whether we use "should" or "could".

I *should* be married. —> Something is wrong with me for not being married.

I *could* be married. —> At my age, many people are married, but I'm not. I may choose to get married at some stage in the future. But

I may also choose not to get married at all if that's not something I want.

I *should* be making more money. —> Something is wrong with me for not being able to make more money. The world is unfair to me.

I *could* be making more money. —> I'm not making as much money as I want right now, but there are things I can do, starting today, that will help me generate more money in the future, such as asking for a raise, changing career or creating my own business.

There *should* be no war. —> Something is wrong with the world. It's a violent place. It should be peaceful.

There *could* be no war. —> If we work toward developing a more peaceful society, perhaps in the future, wars might disappear or occur less frequently.

The bottom line is, in order to develop an accurate model of reality, you must accept that things are exactly the way they're supposed to be right now, whether you like it or not.

This is the first step: accepting reality as it is.

Then once you recognize things are the way they *are*, you can start envisioning a better future and create a blueprint to improve things you wish would be different.

Action step

Complete the following exercises using your action guide:

Write down at least three "should" statements you often use.

Replace "should" with "could".

See how it makes you feel and how it changes your thought process.

Uncovering your assumptions

Identifying your assumptions

Whenever you set a life goal, you immediately start making assumptions regarding what you need to do to achieve it. Your assumptions may be that this goal is unrealistic and that you will never reach it. Or they may suggest that to obtain a specific outcome, you will need to do X, Y or Z.

For instance, let's assume you've written a book and want it to become a best-seller. Your first idea might be to go on national TV. You think you will sell thousands of copies that way. Or perhaps you believe that because you spent so much time and energy writing your book—and care so much about your readers—, it will sell gazillions of copies. It's just a matter of time before people find out about your books, right?

In short, for any of your goals, you will make initial assumptions regarding the best strategy to reach it, but these assumptions will often be inaccurate. Now what do you think will happen if you decide to take action based on these weak assumptions? You'll waste your time and energy and will probably fail to attain your goal. Sadly, this is what many people do, often unknowingly.

The bottom line is, before you start working on any goal, you need to identify all your erroneous assumptions. Then you need to replace them with more accurate ones. The better you become at this "game", the more likely you are to hit your target.

Action step

Using your action guide, select one important goal and make a list of all the assumptions you may be making about it. Please note we'll keep using this goal for future exercises.

To help you identify your assumptions, please refer to the questions below:

- What are your assumptions regarding the best ways to reach this goal?

- What strategies do you assume will work and why?

- Do you think it will be easy or hard, and why?

- How long do you think it will take you to reach this goal and why?

Testing your assumptions

Once you have identified the assumptions you're making regarding your goal, the next step is to assess each one to see how accurate it is. Don't worry if you're unsure about the accuracy of your assumptions. That's normal. As you do more research and gather invaluable information, you'll be able to improve the quality and accuracy of your assumptions. We'll work on this throughout the book, but for now, it's time to work through the assessment process. And remember, there are no wrong answers.

Action step

Look at the list of assumptions you just wrote down in your action guide.

Next to each assumption, write down the accuracy score you would give it on a scale from 1 to 10, (one being completely inaccurate and 10 being one hundred percent accurate).

CHAPTER 12:

Know the truth about yourself

Learn Who You Are

Learning who we truly are has to start with us. Who we are is not determined by others? It's determined by our strengths, personality, experiences, passions, and our ultimate purpose or calling in our lives. That's why when we give into our fears, negative thoughts, or the opinions of others, we limit ourselves from living to our fullest potential.

Strengths

Take the time to ask yourself and others closest to you what your strengths may be. Maybe you already know. This is something you'll want to journal about and add to as necessary. Strengths don't ultimately make us who we are or determine what our purpose is in this life, but they're tools we'll most likely need to use along the way.

Take the time now to list your strengths. Maybe your strengths are strong values or morals that you've never considered strengths before. Maybe they are skills you don't give yourself enough credit for. Ask those closest to you for their insights. Don't be concerned if you think their insight doesn't match up; oftentimes, you're blind to the good things about yourself before you either learn to love yourself or practice using your strengths.

Personality

It's important to note what your personality is like when considering who you are and, ultimately, what your purpose is in this life. Wherever it is, you're sure to thrive.

You need to be able to identify if you're an ***extrovert*** or an ***introvert***, if you prefer ***routine*** or ***variety***, if you're more of a ***thinker*** or a ***feeler***, and if you work better ***individually*** or as part of a ***team***. It's important to grow in areas we're uncomfortable with, but it's also important to know in which circumstances we'll ultimately ***thrive***.

The best personality examples I found for this assignment was when looking at the four temperaments. They're called choleric, sanguine, phlegmatic, and melancholic.

So, what now? I encourage you to search for a test that will identify one of these four temperaments. It also doesn't hurt to look up all four descriptions beforehand to get an idea of which one you might be.

It's important to know who you are because you'll never reach your fullest potential by comparing yourself to others or trying to copy someone else. You can't be the world's best copycat. That's not an accomplishment.

Experiences

What are you going to do with your past experiences? If you've had great ones, are you going to share them with others? If you've had bad past experiences (I can totally identify with this one), how are you going to move through it so that one day you can help others? I believe we're all meant to go through our own struggles so that we can overcome and help others who need encouragement to do so as well. If you're at a dark place right now, I encourage you to keep this in perspective.

Everyone goes through stresses in life; everyone has to learn how to balance their life (or not). One of the most noticeable traits of success we can identify in someone else is when they're balancing their life. Our spirituality, personal development, family relationships, work life, and friendships—they're all a part of this. The question is, if we haven't been doing a good job with managing our time in the past, are we going to start today? Our past experiences don't have to define our today or our tomorrow.

This is why it's especially important to let go of any beliefs or expectations we have regarding our life based on our past experiences. This can be difficult. If we listen to our negative voice telling us, "What makes you think you can do that? You've never done that before," we'll never create the life we want for ourselves. If we look at our current relationships and expect to be treated the same way we were treated in our past relationships, we'll never have healthy relationships.

One of the most important things you can do for yourself if you're living in the past (which is called regret) is to forgive where you need to forgive.

If you're beating yourself up, forgive yourself. If you're holding a grudge, forgive whomever it is. Forgiveness isn't for the other person. It's for your own inner peace. Forgiveness is not equivalent to trust, either.

Forgiveness can be instant, but trust must be earned. Don't confuse the two and think that if you forgive someone, you have to let them back into your life or even confront them with it.

Forgiveness can be as simple as speaking it to your own spirit. It's releasing the control that resentment, bitterness, and anger have over your life.

Passions

Think back to when you were a kid. What were you passionate about? What was your pretend play often centered around? What did you love to do? What activities did you prefer doing? What were you great at? What did you get compliments for? What were your interactions like with others? Whom did you connect with? What do you stand for?

Purpose – Consult Your Creator and Reflect on Your Fears

So, you could do these one of two ways. I'll mention the easiest and (in my opinion) least accurate attempt at figuring out your purpose first.

You can look at all of your strengths, experiences, passions, and, taking into account your personality, think of a career you could pursue to meet all of these needs. It seems difficult, but, believe me, it can be done. Maybe pick something that enables you to give back to other people somehow. This would fill your fulfillment tank, so to speak.

However, if you're a believer in Christ, He hasn't just created you. He has also called you to a specific purpose. If this is your avenue, it will take the step above, but it will also take quiet time with your Creator to know your calling. When we quiet our minds and focus on God's heart, he reveals things to us we would have otherwise missed. This is true communion with God. This is what building a relationship with Christ means.

CHAPTER 13:

Identify your goals

Why You Need Goals

Chances are good you already have some goals in life. Maybe you want to get a promotion at work, lose ten pounds, or travel to Singapore.

Having goals is important for many reasons, but sometimes your limiting beliefs can affect the things you see as goals.

What does goals do for us?

It gives us something to strive for

Without concrete goals, many people can get bogged down and stop moving forward with their lives. When you are working toward something, it keeps you motivated and energetic.

It tells you what you really want

A lot of times, you might feel unsure about what you desire from life.

When you set a goal for yourself, though, it serves as a reminder of what is important to you – what you value.

It keeps you accountable for mistakes and failures

We all make mistakes, but that can be a good thing if we are willing to learn from them. Goals help keep you on track – when you have a clear goal, you can hold yourself accountable for things you do wrong and take steps to correct your errors.

It makes big tasks seem achievable

Sometimes you might have a really big goal, one that seems impossible. When you break a large goal down into smaller goals, those smaller steps can seem easier to take than they would if you just focused on the long-term goal.

It makes it easier for you to believe in yourself

When you set goals for yourself, you are telling yourself that you think you can achieve them. The belief that you can do something often has a huge effect on whether or not you will do it.

Having goals is necessary if you want to grow as a person. If you have nothing to strive for, you may find yourself simply going through the motions in life like I was. When your life becomes stagnant, the stagnation can spread. You can start to think that you can never change anything, and that is especially damaging.

How Limiting Beliefs Affect Your Goals

Today's exercise is about setting goals, as you may have guessed. Before we talk about what you need to do, let's first take a moment to discuss the way the limiting beliefs you identified yesterday might be affecting the goals you set for yourself. Let's look at a common goal as an example. Many people want to lose a few pounds, and they have goals for losing weight, eating healthier, and exercising more. Their goals might be modest (I want to lose ten pounds before my high school reunion) or ambitious (I am severely overweight, and I need to lose a hundred pounds for my health.) I guarantee, though, that the people who are successful at losing weight are the ones who believe they can do it.

Instead of saying "I can't lose weight," they are saying, "I can lose weight."

Instead of saying "I am fat," they are saying, "I am carrying some extra weight now, but it doesn't have to be that way."

Instead of saying "Other people lose weight easily, but I don't," they are saying, "If other people can do it, I can too!"

Do you see the difference? When you move beyond your limiting beliefs and eliminate them from your goal-setting process, you make it much more likely that you will shoot for the stars – and reach them.

Goal Setting Exercise

You need goals, and today's exercise is going to help you set some new goals for yourself, without being shackled by your limiting beliefs.

To start, write down a list of your current goals. When you look at those goals, do you see any ways in which your limiting beliefs are holding you back? For example, deep down, do you want to be a doctor, but you've told yourself you are going to get a nursing degree because you think it's easier? Make notes of anything about your current goals that you feel is impacted by your limiting beliefs.

Once you have that list, I want you to make a new list of goals – and when you write it, I want you to banish those limiting beliefs from your goal-making process completely. Every time you write down a goal, revisit your list of limiting beliefs and rewrite the goal until it is as big as it needs to be. Don't worry about what you think you can or can't do, or what you think is realistic. This exercise is not about being realistic; it's about aiming for the sky. I'm not suggesting that you give over your life to something that is truly not achievable, such as sprouting a pair of wings and flying – but it is important to be ambitious here. Once you have your list of goals, the next step is to break each one down into achievable mini goals. Let's use weight loss as an example again. If you want to lose one hundred pounds, your goal might look like this:

Goal: Lose 100 pounds

Daily goal: Keep track of food intake, limit sugar, exercise 30 minutes

Weekly goal: Weigh in once a week, aim for two pounds of weight loss per week

Monthly goal: Take body measurements, try one new exercise.

Six-month goal: Learn how to cook one new healthy recipe a week, increase daily exercise by 25 mins, buy smaller clothes.

One-year goal: Reach goal weight, celebrate.

You get the idea. It is important to break down each goal into more easily achievable sections. If you are just thinking about your end goal – losing 100 pounds – you might feel as if it's impossible. But when you break it down like this, you give yourself a better chance of success. You're telling yourself that it is possible.

Conclusion

Shifting limiting beliefs is something that people can struggle with. At the core, shifting a belief simply comes down to a decision that you will no longer believe this belief because it is disempowering, and doesn't serve you, and choosing a new belief instead. What I wrote here will hopefully help you navigate that transition.

The more you begin to understand about the law of attraction, the more deeply it will sink in, your beliefs are what created your experiences. You will come to see they are not some absolute truth, about how things are. This will aid you in the release.

If you try to buy into beliefs that just seem too far from where you are now, nothing is going to change, and you are just going to feel worse.

Whatever beliefs you have now that make you think you can't have what you want, are just that...beliefs. They are not fact. They can be changed. Remember there is a reason they feel so badly--this is your emotional guidance system letting you know that they are bullshit.